Insalata Italiana:

The Italian Salad Cookbook

Antonio Marchesi

Introduction 1

Know The Ingredients 2

Fruits and Vegetables 3
Useful Cooking Techniques For Vegetables 16
Blanching Vegetables 16
Grilling Vegetables 17
Roasting Vegetables 17
Sautéing Vegetables 18

Herbs, Spices, and Seasonings 18

Olive Oil, Vinegar, and Condiments 19
Olive Oil Basics 20
Vinegar Basics 22
Condiments 23

Cheese 24

Pasta 25
Fresh Pasta 26
Stuffed Fresh Pasta Shapes 38
Dried Pasta 44
Egg Pasta 45
Preparing, Saucing, and Serving Pasta 46

Rice, Seeds, Grains, and Bread 48

Fish and Seafood 50

Meat 51

Wine, Beer, and Other Drinks 52
Wine 52
Beer 53
Coffee 54

Basic Italian Cooking Techniques 55
General Tips 55
Tools 57
Cooking Methods 58

Measurements for Non-US Cooks 61

Appetizers 63
Artichoke and Mint Frittata 65

Baked Clams Oreganata	66
Baked Eggplant and Eggs	67
Baked Eggs With White Truffles	69
Baked Mushroom Crostini	71
Calf's Brain In A Lemon Sauce	72
Celery Stalks Stuffed With Gorgonzola and Apples	74
Cheese Baked In A Crust	75
Chicken Liver Crostini	76
Clams Casino	77
Egg-Battered Zucchini Roll-Ups	79
Eggplant Rollatini	81
Eggs Poached In Tomato Sauce	83
Eggs Scrambled In Tomato Sauce	85
Fava and Sesame Dip	86
Frico With Montasio Cheese and Apples	87
Frico With Montasio Cheese and Potatoes	89
Lentil Crostini	91
Lettuce and Bread Quiches	92
Mussels In Spicy Tomato Sauce	94
Prosciutto and Fig Bruschetta	96
Provolone Turnovers	97
Rice and Zucchini Crostata	99
Rice Balls	102
Ricotta Frittata	104
Roasted Pepper Rolls Stuffed With Tuna	105
Rosemary and Lemon Focaccia	107
Sausage Crostini	112
Sausage, Bread, and Pepper Frittata	113
Scrambled Eggs and Asparagus	115
Steamed Mussels In Savory Wine Sauce	115
Stuffed Artichokes	117
Stuffed Mushrooms	119
Stuffed Olives Ascolane	121
Stuffed Zucchini Blossoms	123
Swiss Chard and Potato Crostata	125
Swordfish-Stuffed Peppers	127
Tomato Fritters	129
Whipped Salt Cod Spread	130
Zucchini Fritters	132

Salads *134*

Caesar Salad	134

Celery Root, Apple, Arugula, and Walnut Salad 136
Celery, Artichoke, and Mortadella Salad 137
Condiggion Salad with Tuna 139
Crab and Celery Salad 140
Cucumber, Potato, and Green Bean Salad 141
Farro Salad with Grilled Eggplant and Peppers 142
Lobster Salad with Fresh Tomatoes 144
Octopus and Potato Salad 146
Pickled Carrots 148
Poached Seafood Salad 149
Puntarelle and Anchovy Salad 151
Radicchio Salad with Orange 153
Raw and Cooked Salad 154
Red Cabbage and Bacon Salad 156
Roasted Beet and Beet Greens Salad with Apples and Goat Cheese 157
Roasted Eggplant and Tomato Salad 159
Salad of Dandelion Greens with Almond Vinaigrette and Dried Ricotta 161
Scallion and Asparagus Salad 162
Seafood and Rice Salad 164
Shaved Fennel, Celery, and Red Onion Salad with Salami 167
Shrimp and Mixed Bean Salad 168
Steamed Broccoli and Egg Salad 169
Striped Bass Salad 170
Tomato and Bread Salad 171
Tripe Salad 172
Warm Mushroom Salad 174

Endnote 176

Introduction

Food is probably the most important part of an average Italian's life. Born and brought up in Naples, a city in southern Italy, I experienced the Italian food culture firsthand. My mom and dad were both amazing cooks, and both had their favorite dishes they loved to cook. My love for cooking started watching my parents cook together. No matter how the day went, my parents would always have a blast in the kitchen, and even more so the dinner table. When I grew tall enough to reach most of the shelves in out kitchen, I joined in on the fun and started helping out with the cooking process. A few years of cooking with my parents, and I was ready to experiment with what my parents had taught me, and started creating my own recipes.

Today, I own a small restaurant in Naples, and write Italian cookbooks on the side. Cooking will always be my passion, but sharing my recipes with the world is even more fun! There is nothing more fun than helping people who have only ever had Italian food in restaurants experience the joy of cooking and eating authentic Italian food, right at home, as that is the way Italian food was always meant to be enjoyed: homecooked, with family and friends. Don't get me wrong, most Italian restaurants make insanely delicious Italian food, but cooking the food is most of the fun, and you're basically paying those restaurants to have fun at your expense. Don't let them have all the fun, and save some for yourself. A few good Italian recipes are absolutely indispensable for the arsenal of any home cook, and since you have picked up this book, I'll arm you to the teeth.

Italian recipes are some of the simplest recipes to prepare, so even if you're a newb at cooking, you will be able to cook the recipes in this book with good success. If Italian cooking is completely new to you, you will do well to learn about some of the popular ingredients and cooking techniques before we jump into the recipes. The following sections do exactly that.

KNOW THE INGREDIENTS

If you want to cook authentic Italian food, you will first need to source authentic Italian ingredients. Non-authentic ingredients will do in a pinch, but if you're serious about Italian cooking, you would do well to include a few of the Italian staples in your kitchen pantry.

When buying Italian food products, watch the label for the following few abbreviations that ensure that you're buying authentic Italian ingredients.

DOP, or Denominazione di Origine Protetta, is a mark endorsed by the European Community to promote and ensures that the food or agricultural product you are looking at is authentic, and that it represents the designated geographical area for that product.

IGP, Indicazione Geografica Protetta, applies to agricultural products and foods whose qualities derive from the growth and transformation of a specific area.

DOCG, Denominazione di Origine Controllata e Garantita, applies to wine-production zones and determines specific wine-growing zones, making sure that a specific wine is produced from officially prescribed grapes or blend of grapes.

FRUITS AND VEGETABLES

Vegetables and legumes are easily one of the most important ingredients in Italian cuisine. Vegetables and legumes might not be the first things to come to mind when you think of Italian food, but they are responsible for most of the flavour and color of Italian food.

Fruits are naturally sweet, and are an indispensable part of Italian desserts, and many other dishes. Make sure the fruits are fresh and ripe before you use in a recipe. Fruits that are in season are preferred.

Fruits and vegetables should be thoroughly washed before use, and used immediately after cutting. If you have to store them, store them properly. Depending on the fruit or vegetable, there is an ideal way to store it. For example, onions and potatoes should be stored in cool dark places. Broccoli and spinach should always be refrigerated. The best way to store fresh herbs is in a damp towel, or in a container filled with water.

ALMONDS

Almonds are a staple in the Italian pantry, and a common ingredient in some of the most popular Italian recipes and desserts. Sicily is revered for its almonds, and its almond dished.

APPLES

Italians love to eat apples raw, and also used them in desserts and salads. Applesauce is a great ingredient for low-fat baking.

ARTICHOKES

Italy is the biggest producer and exporter of artichokes in the world, and artichokes are an indispensable part of Italian cuisine. These are used in all kinds of Italian recipes.

ARUGULA

Arugula is a flavourful, peppery salad green of the mustard family that is an important ingredient in Italian cuisine and grows wild all over the Mediterranean. It is a popular ingredient in salads, sandwiches, frittatas, sauces, etc.

ASPARAGUS

Green asparagus is the most common kind used in Italian cuisine. If you can't find it, white or purple asparagus will do just fine.

BEETS

Beets are in season from March to October, so it is best to cook recipes calling for beets during this time. These are vital ingredients for risotto, salads, soups, etc.

BELL PEPPERS

Peppers come in all shapes, sizes, and taste. When it comes to Italian cooking, we mostly use the sweet kinds of bell peppers. Sweet bell peppers also come in multiple colors, but all colors taste pretty much the same. As a general rule, the brighter colored bell peppers are sweeter. When buying these, make sure you buy fresh ones with tight skin. Never pick shriveled ones.

Quite a few recipes in this book will require you to roast peppers. Roasting enhances flavour and makes the skin easy to remove. Here's how it is done:

Use long tongs to place the peppers directly over the flame of your stove, and roast until blackened on all sides, flipping them over as needed. Approximately 8 minutes. Take the blackened peppers off the heat and put them in a container, covering the container firmly using plastic wrap. Allow to sit until cool enough to handle. Chop the peppers in two along the length and allow the seeds and juices to flow out. Scrape away the black skin, ribs, and any leftover seeds. Give the bell peppers a quick rinse in water if there are still some seeds and black skin sticking to the peppers.

BROCCOLI

In Italian, the word *broccoli* stands for "cabbage sprout." This is a highly popular ingredient all over the world and needs no introduction. When buying broccoli, check to make sure there are no yellowish buds on it, as this means the broccoli is past its prime.

BROCCOLI RABE

Called rapini in Italy, broccoli rabe is an Italian staple and cooked in multiple ways. Most commonly, it is used in vegetable sides, appetizers, pasta dressings, and sandwiches.

BRUSSELS SPROUTS

If handled and cooked right, brussels sprouts greatly enhance the flavour of food, and are a common ingredient in Italian cuisine. These go great on the side with Italian meat dishes. Buy them fresh and firm, when they are still bright green in colour.

CABBAGE

Cabbage is a common ingredient in Italian salads, sauerkraut, pasta sauces, etc. It is insanely nutritious and if cooked right, insanely delicious too.

CAPERS

Caper berries are crunchy, acidic, and have s strong flavour. They are a common ingredient in Italian antipasto, salads, sauces, etc.

CARDOONS

Cardoons are well known in all parts of the world, but they are absolutely indispensable for Italian cooking. These take some patience to work with, but the result is worth it.

CARROTS

Carrots are a common ingredient in Italian recipes. They are commonly used in soups, and are also enjoyed boiled, raw, fried, or puréed. Always buy fresh organic carrots with the greens still attached to them so you get an idea of how fresh they are.

CAULIFLOWER

Commonly enjoyed raw in Italian salads, cauliflower is commonly cooked by steaming, baking, blanching, or sautéing. Make sure you buy it fresh, without any yellow spots. It is mostly tasteless, and super nutritious.

CELERY

This cheap and delicious vegetable is one of the most underrated vegetables out there. It is commonly used in Italian soups and meaty salads.

CELERY ROOT

This root is peeled and used in Italian salads, stews, etc. It tastes great when mashed with potatoes.

CHERRIES

A common ingredient in Italian recipes, cherries are nutritious and loaded with vitamins. They have anti-inflammatory properties too! They come in wide varieties of sweetness and color.

CHICKPEAS

Also known as garbanzo beans, chickpeas are commonly grown in Southern parts of Italy and are a staple in the Italian kitchen. They are enjoyed to make pasta sauces and soups. Chickpea flour is a common ingredient for breads and pastries. They are inexpensive, and great for health!

CRANBERRIES

Although these are not common in classic Italian recipes, cranberries are only now gaining popularity in Italy. This versatile ingredient is now being used by cooks all over Italy.

EDIBLE FLOWERS

Quite a few vegetables we eat today are actually edible flowers. Artichokes are a great example of this, although they don't really seem like flowers. However, there are flowers like viola that seem like flowers, and can be eaten directly too! Quite a few Italian cooks use these flowers for garnishing, and most people don't eat these, for most people aren't used to eating flowers. These flowers make for a great garnish, just make sure these are free of pesticides, or you can even grow you own!

EGGPLANT

Eggplants are available in a wide spectrum of shapes and sizes. The eggplant used in Italian cuisine is usually dark purple and evenly elongated. When buying this, make sure the skin is smooth, tight, and shiny. Poached eggplant is a common ingredient, and to poach it, you need to cut the eggplant in sections along the length, and poach it in liquid that is ¾ water and ¼ red wine vinegar.

ESCAROLE

Part of the endive family, escarole is in season during the cold months. The center leaves are light green in color and soft, and go great in salads. The outer tougher leaves are usually eaten sautéed or braised with oil and garlic, or used in soups.

FAVA BEANS

When buying these, make sure they are firm, containing fully ripe beans, and with little to no discoloration. If you won't want to go through the hassle of shelling them, you can buy shelled beans from the market, for a bit more money.

FENNEL

This vegetable is crispy when raw, and soft and sweet when braised or roasted. It is a common herb in classic Italian recipes.

FIDDLEHEAD FERNS

These are highly seasonal, and a common ingredient in pesto, risotto, morels, etc.

FRESH BEANS

Dried beans do the job, and are available throughout the year. However, when the beans are in season, they can be obtained fresh, and are used to make some insanely delicious Italian recipes.

GARLIC

Italian recipes have always contained garlic, but after getting influenced by American recipes, garlic is an even more dominant presence.

GREEN BEANS

Green beans come in hundreds of varieties, each with a different shape, size, and taste. A huge variety of these is used in Italian recipes, and hence are an important part of the Italian pantry. The are diverse, and used in a wide array of Italian recipes.

KALE

Kale is an insanely delicious and nutritious winter vegetable. It is a strong antioxidant and anti-inflammatory agent. It is easy to cook, and used in soups, vegetable dishes, and pasta condiments.

LEEKS

Leeks belong to the onion family, and are usually sweet and mellow compared to yellow and Spanish onions. These make great side dishes and appetizers.

LEMONS

There is no limit to what you can do with lemons, and Italian cooking uses these in a wide variety of recipes. If you want to go for authenticity, get the Sorrento lemon variety, which is an Italian favorite. In a pinch, any old kind of lemon will do.

LENTILS

These dried seeds are nutritious and delicious, and used in a all kinds of Italian recipes!

MUSHROOMS/WILD MUSHROOMS

Buy fresh and firm mushrooms always. Don't soak them in water for too long, and so a quick rinse if they are dirty. Preparing them is quite simple too, just chop off any rigid parts before cooking. The white domestically cultivated mushrooms commonly available in the market will do the job, but if you can, try to get your hands on porcini, chanterelles, morels, or wild varieties.

NETTLES

These require some delicate handling due to the needle-like hair on it. However, if you can get past that minor inconvenience, the reward is totally worth it.

ONIONS

Onions are a staple in food from pretty much every country, and Italian food is no exception. Pretty much all kinds of onions are used in Italian cooking, and the kind of onion used may change with the kind of recipe being cooked. Most recipes specify the kind of onion used, but if not mentioned, use the common yellow onions.

ORANGES

Oranges are one of the most common fruits available all over the world, and Italy is no exception. This acidic citrus fruit is used in a wide array of Italian recipes and drinks.

PEAS

Peas are insanely nutritious, and a staple in the Italian kitchen. Make sure you buy these while they are still fresh and firm.

POTATOES

One of the cheapest and tastiest food available all over the world, potatoes hold an important place in Italian cooking. Potatoes are available in many varieties, and almost all these varieties are used in Italian recipes.

PRUNES

Used to cook sweet and savory Italian recipes, prunes are extremely popular in Italy in the dried form.

RADICCHIO

Tasting sweet and bitter simultaneously, radicchio is a common ingredient in Italian salads, sauces, risotto, and much more!

RAISINS

Dehydrated grapes are a common ingredient all over the world, and Italy is no exception. These can be reconstituted by soaking them in water. If you want to get creative, try soaking them in other liquids. Rum works great if you're thinking of baking these!

RAMPS

Also called wild leeks, ramps have a garlicky sweet flavour, and are used in a wide variety of Italian recipes. They are in season during spring, so make sure you make most of the season!

RHUBARB

Perfect for making chutneys and some sweet dishes like pies, rhubarb imparts a tarty and fruity flavour to the recipes it is used in.

ROMAINE LETTUCE

Not a traditional ingredient, romaine lettuce is comparatively modern addition to the Italian cuisine. This long-leaf lettuce is crunchy and soft at the same time.

SCALLIONS

Also known as green onions or spring onions, scallions are a part of the onion family, and a common ingredient in Italian recipes.

STRAWBERRIES

When strawberries are in season, make sure you cook a lot of Italian recipes that call for them!

SWISS CHARD

A taller and larger version of spinach, swiss chard is insanely nutritious, and used in a wide array of Italian recipes.

TOMATOES

Tomatoes are used in pretty much every Italian recipe... pretty much. I can write a whole book about Italian recipes using tomato. A few of the common Italian tomatoes are: the Pomodorino del Piennolo, Roma, San Marzano, and the Costoluto Genovese. Tomatoes are mostly used crushed, or made into a paste.

TRUFFLES

Truffles can be costly, but are totally worth it. They have s strong distinct aroma, and are used in quite a few Italian recipes

TURNIPS

Turnips are delicious and nutritious, and play an important role in Italian cooking. Turnips can be cooked in a variety of ways, and are hence used in a wide spectrum of recipes.

WINTER SQUASH

Winter Squash is slowly gaining popularity in Italian cuisine, and used in quite a few Italian recipes these days.

ZUCCHINI

These are cheap, and easily available all over the world. Zucchini is used in all kinds of Italian recipes, and should be a staple in the pantry of anyone looking to cook Italian food.

USEFUL COOKING TECHNIQUES FOR VEGETABLES

Vegetables are the most important ingredient in Italian cooking, and there are a few cooking techniques you will be using a lot when cooking vegetables the Italian way. Always buy fresh vegetables that are in season, and always check for blemishes. There is an ideal way to store every vegetable. Google it if you're unsure of how to store a particular vegetable you wish to store. Let us now look at some of the commonly used techniques in a little more detail.

Blanching Vegetables

Here's how you blanch vegetables:

1. Quickly boil the vegetables.
2. Drain.
3. Toss with medium-coarse salt while still scorching hot.
4. Toss them into ice water to stop from cooking further. (not necessary)

This simple process the vegetables retain their color, texture, nutrients, and taste. You can blanch them in salted water, but plain water is preferable. You can always salt them after boiling.

Grilling Vegetables

Here's how you grill vegetables:

1. Chop up the vegetable you wish to grill into equally sized pieces so they finish cooking at the same time. Small pieces cook faster.
2. Clean the grilling surface and lightly coat it with oil to prevent sticking.
3. Brush the seasoning and oil onto the vegetables.
4. Wrap the vegetables in heavy-duty foil and grill.
5. Take the vegetables off the grill before they become too soft.
6. Allow them to stay in the foil for a while longer, as they continue to cook during this time.

The time you will need to cook them for will vary with the kind of vegetable. If you're new to this process, you might overcook or undercook them, but you will get used to the timing eventually.

Roasting Vegetables

Some vegetables like squashes peppers, tomatoes, eggplants, etc. taste great roasted. Roasting greatly enhances the flavour of the vegetable. Here's how It is done:

1. Preheat your oven to 400 degrees.
2. Chop the vegetables as you wish.

3. Coat a baking sheet with parchment paper and lay the chopped vegetables on the sheet.
4. Season with salt, pepper, and other herbs to taste.
5. Roast in oven until fairly shriveled and caramelized on all sides.

Sautéing Vegetables

You can do this directly, or blanch the vegetables before you sauté. Here's how it is done.

1. Chop up the vegetables into equally sized pieces.
2. Take a frying pan and put some olive oil and garlic into them.
3. Turn on the heat, and once the oil is hot, throw the vegetable pieces into the pan.
4. Sprinkle with seasoning and stir/toss intermittently until cooked.

Herbs, Spices, and Seasonings

Herbs, spices, and seasonings should be a staple in every kitchen, Italian or not. But when it comes to Italian cooking, thy are absolutely indispensable. If you wish to cook Italian recipes on a regular basis, you will do well to stock your kitchen up with the following:

- Basil

- Bay leaves
- Cinnamon
- Cloves
- Marjoram
- Mint
- Nutmeg
- Oregano
- Parsley
- Peperoncino/crushed red pepper
- Peppercorns
- Rosemary
- Saffron
- Sage
- Salt
- Sugar
- Thyme

Olive Oil, Vinegar, and Condiments

Olive oil and vinegar are indispensable for your pantry if you wish to cook Italian food. Both these ingredients are usually used uncooked, especially when used as dressings. A wide variety of olives are grown all over Italy, and this leads to a wide variety of olive oils too. Below, we will take a detailed look at these Ingredients.

Olive Oil Basics

The grade of olive oil—extra-virgin, virgin, etc.—that appears on each bottle's label is based on the residual oleic acid. The less acidic an olive oil is, the better its quality.

- EXTRA-VIRGIN OLIVE OIL (EVOO) has no more than 1 percent oleic acid.
- VIRGIN OLIVE OIL contains from 1 to 3.3 percent oleic acid.
- PLAIN OLIVE OIL has an acidity level higher than 3.3 percent.
- OLIVE POMACE OIL is the oil extracted from olive pomace (crushed olives and pits) using solvents; this oil is then purified and combined with virgin olive oil.
- OLIO NOVELLO is newly pressed olive oil, normally less than two months old. It is vibrant green in color, very vegetal, fresh in flavor, and sometimes slightly murky, with little particles of pulp.

Olive oils are also categorized on the basis of region, but in most cases any old olive oil you can get your hands on will get the job done.

HOW TO USE OLIVE OIL

Olive oil is an Italian staple, and highly nutritious. It is a strong antioxidant. Extra-virgin olive oil is best when used raw, right out of the bottle, to sprinkle on salads and before you serve soup or pasta. You get the most flavour out of your olive-oil this way. Do not use olive oil for frying—canola or vegetable oil is best—but you can put in a little olive oil to the pan for flavor. You can use olive oil for other kinds of cooking and sautéing, but it is best when you are cooking at a lower temperature.

TESTING OLIVE OIL

With so many brands of olive oil available today, testing them to identify the best one is a good way to go.

The first thing to check is colour. Riper olives usually make yellowish olive oil, while younger olives make a greener olive oil which also has stronger flavour. If the oil is freshly pressed, it has a very prominent green colour. As it ages, the prominence of green weakens.

The next thing to do is to smell it. It should smell fresh, and then taste it. The taste should match the smell and should not feel heavy or greasy in the mouth.

GARLIC-INFUSED OIL

This is a handy little oil to have in your pantry if you wish to cook Italian food on a regular basis. You can make your own by putting three finely chopped slices of garlic for each cup of EVOO. Strain, pout into an air-tight bottle and store in your fridge.

HOLY OIL

This is a southern Italian specialty, also called *olio santo.* This oil is spicy and hot, and a great addition to recipes if you like your recipes hot. Here's how you make it:

1. Pour a cup of good-quality extra-virgin olive oil into a glass jar, and drop in a teaspoon of kosher salt and two tablespoons of small, whole dried peperoncini, approximately ten little peppers.
2. Cover firmly, and let the oil infuse at room temperature for minimum two days.
3. Shake thoroughly, and use. Store in a sealed jar, in a cool place, for at least one month.

UNCOOKED OLIVE OIL SAUCE

A quick and delicious sauce that makes for a spectacular dressing. Making this is really simple: all you require is good-quality olive oil, garlic cloves, hot pepper, fresh herbs of your choice, nuts of your choice, and whatever else you want to put in there.

Crush the ingredients using a mortar and pestle and you're done.

Vinegar Basics

Vinegar is another ingredient you should always have on hand if you wish to cook Italian recipes on a regular basis. There are vinegars of all kinds made from all kinds of fruits, vegetables, nuts, grains, etc. When it comes to Italian cooking, some of the popular vinegars are: red and white wine, apple, balsamic, and Saba vinegar. Below are two of the labels to watch for:

ACETO BALSAMICO TRADIZIONALE

A classic balsamic vinegar made using traditional method of production, which involves seven years in wooden barrels of different sizes and types of woods. The vinegar so labeled is far superior and is quite costly too. Aceto Balsamico Tradizionale is perfect when used without cooking; sprinkle it on grilled steaks, salads, cheeses, fruit, ice cream, etc.

ACETO BALSAMICO COMMERCIALE

This vinegar is a mix of the vinegar we talked about above, and vinegar aged in big oak casks. The proportions of the mixtures can vary, and taste can vary depending on the proportions. This vinegar is best to cook with.

Condiments

Certain condiments are highly popular in Italian cooking and we will take a look at the most popular ones in this section.

CHUTNEY

These are flavour, usually quite spicy sauces of Indian origin. These are almost always made fresh using raw ingredients. Italian versions of chutneys usually contain vinegar too. These are easy to make, and make for great sides with pretty much every main course.

HONEY

Honey is another Italian staple that is enjoyed all over Italy. Honey is available in many flavours, depending on the flower the bees were made to collect from. Popular Italian honeys are made from thyme, sage, acacia, lavender, and many more.

MOSTARDA

This is a condiment made using candied fruits and mustard syrup, and has always been an important component of the Italian pantry.

CHEESE

We Italians love our cheese. More than 460 kinds of cheese are produced in Italy! You don't need to know about all of them though. Below are some of the most popular varieties used in the recipes in this book. If you can't find these in a nearby store, you can always get them online on amazon.

- Asiago
- Bel paese
- Burrata
- Caciocavallo
- Caprino
- Castelmagno

- Fontina
- Gorgonzola
- Grana padano
- Mascarpone
- Montasio
- Mozzarella
- Parmigiano-reggiano
- Pecorino
- Provolone
- Ricotta
- Scamorza
- Taleggio

Pasta

Pasta is probably the second thing that comes to mind when someone mentions Italian food, the first probably being Pizza. You can buy pasta either fresh or dried. Fresh pasta is moist and tender, made using a wide variety of flours and other ingredients. Dried pasta is usually made using durum-wheat flour and water, and then dried completely. Both kinds of pasta come in all shapes and sizes, and are used in more kinds recipes I can think of.

Both fried and fresh pasta have their pros and cons, and cooking techniques for both are different. Fresh pasta is more time consuming and involved process as compared to the dry version, but it tastes better so the effort is worth it. I remember making fresh pasta with my parents ages ago, and absolutely enjoyed the process. Try making fresh pasta with your family sometime, and thank me later. Let us take a look at the most popular kinds of pastas in a little more detail below.

Fresh Pasta

DOUGH CONSISTENCY

If you have a food processor, it will serve you well to make fresh pasta dough. You can also do it by hand if you don't have one, but it is not recommended for beginners. Remember to elt the dough sit for at least half an hour before you roll it. Once rolled, you can cut the pasta into a shape of your choice, and cook it as soon as possible.

EGGS AND HOMEMADE PASTA

Eggs are an important ingredient of pasta dough. How many eggs you put in it is really up to your preference, or budget. An all-egg-yolk fresh pasta is ultra-rich, but not everyone will like how it tastes. As a beginner, I will advise you to take the middle approach and make good blend of flour, a couple of eggs, some extra virgin olive oil, and water. There are no right proportions of this. Everyone has a different preference. The only way to find out what works for you is to just go ahead and make it once, and tweak the ingredients little by little every time, until you hit the perfect spot. Feel free to completely omit eggs and oil from the mixture too, if you're on a diet.

FRESH PASTA WITH NUTS

Toast your favorite nuts whole, and grind them using a food processor until tiny bits of desired size are achieved. Don't grind them into a powder. Usually, particles of a couple of millimeters in size do the job. Remove any bigger particles and eat them. Add these ground nuts to your dough and fold the dough to mix.

GRAIN PASTA

Milled grains, finely ground seeds, nuts, and dried beans can be mixed with all-purpose flour to obtain pasta dough. A few of the commonly used doughs out here in Italy are: whole-wheat, chestnut, buckwheat, semolina, and many other such flours. Depending on the type and amount of flour used, a wide variety of pasta flours with different tastes and textures can be obtained.

HOW TO STORE FRESH PASTA

Fresh pasta is not really made to be stored. If you can, never make it in advance, and cook all the fresh pasta immediately after you've made it. If you've prepared some extra by mistake, you can store it in your freezer. But try not to have to store it. Fresh pasta is meant to be enjoyed fresh.

FRESH PASTA SHAPES

BIGOLI

Usually made with whole-wheat flour, they are thick and have a chewy texture. These are made by pushing the pasta dough through a pasta press.

CAVATELLI

Cylinders made using durum flour, rolled, then dragged across a wooden board to make the indentation.

FREGNACCE

Made in Lazio and Abruzzo, an egg-pasta dough rolled thin and sliced into lozenge (rhombus diamond) shapes.

FREGOLA

Made by sprinkling water little by little, gradually over flour and mixing the dough around using hands until small kernels of wet flour are achieved; they are strained and then given time to dry. Commonly cooked in broth as a kind of pastina.

GARGANELLI

Made of fresh dough that is rolled into a slim sheet, then sliced into rhombus diamonds; two ends are then folded into the middle onto each other, and pinched together.

MACCHERONI ALLA CHITARRA

An egg-dough pasta from Abruzzo, rolled into slim sheets and then pressed against the rigid strings of a special "chitarra," a wooden box with strings like a guitar, and rolled over using a small rolling pin, so the dough separates into long strands. The texture of pasta made with this tool is something not achievable by other means.

MACCHERONI AL TORCHIO

A durum-flour pasta made using a hand press, varying in shape and size depending on the die used in the press.

MALTAGLIATI

Literally meaning "poorly or badly cut"; long sheets of dough are rolled out, and the dough is cut into irregular rhombus shapes.

ORECCHIETTE

The literal meaning of the word is "little ears." It is usually made using Durum-wheat pasta dough. To make it, first mix and knead the dough, and then pinch off little pieces off the dough and roll them into long cylinders looking like pencils. Little pieces are cut from these strands of rolled dough, which are then pressed down against a wooden board and lightly dragged using a blunt knife. One side has a textured surface because of the wooden board, and the other side has a minor indentation as the dough rolls up due to being dragged along the board.

PAPPARDELLE

Fresh egg dough rolled out into slim sheets, then cut into long ribbons, approximately 1½ inches wide.

PASSATELLI

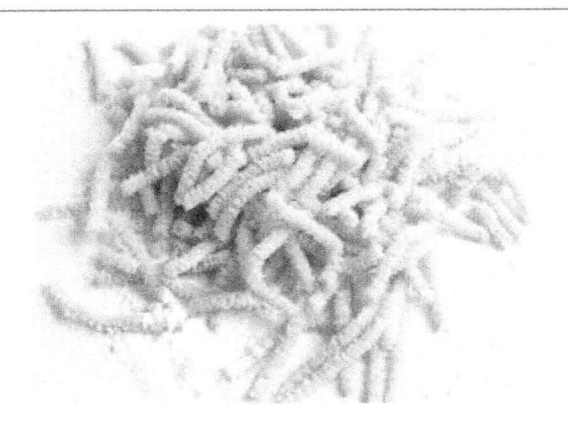

A thick spaghetti-like pasta made out of bread crumbs, eggs, cheese, lemon, nutmeg, and parsley. It is usually made by pressing the dough through tiny holes of something like a perforated heavy-duty sheet.

PICI

One of the easiest pastas to make, PICI can be made by individually rolling pieces of dough by hand into four-to-five-inch spaghetti-like shapes.

PIZZOCCHERI

These thick noodles are made using using buckwheat flour mixed with wheat flour and water.

SCIALATIELLI

To make these, simply roll the dough into a sheet and cut it into long flat noodles.

SFOGLIA

Literally meaning "sheet", this dough is made is simply made by mixing wheat, eggs and water, and then rolling it out into a sheet.

SPAETZLE

The dough is made by combining flour, water, and some milk, and then pressed through a porous utensil directly into boiling water or soup.

STRASCINATI

To make this, pinch off fresh dough pieces and roll them into cylindrical strands using your hands. After that, cut into small pieces, approximately an inch and a half long. Drag these pieces of dough across a wooden board, by finger or using a tool, so that an indentation is achieved.

STROZZAPRETI

Basically, this is fresh pasta rolled and formed into a twisted and elongated form.

TACCONI

Made using corn flour, wheat flour, and water, this dough is rolled out, and strips about one inch wide are cut, and then cut once more into a rhombus shape.

TROFIE

Wheat-flour pasta dough usually combined with riced potato or chestnut flour. Pieces about 1½ inches long are pinched off the dough and rolled using hands, and then twisting a little.

Stuffed Fresh Pasta Shapes

In this section, we will take a look at a few of the most common shapes of stuffed fresh pasta.

AGNOLOTTI

A rectangular, ridged-edge shape; commonly filled with mixed meat filling.

ANOLINI

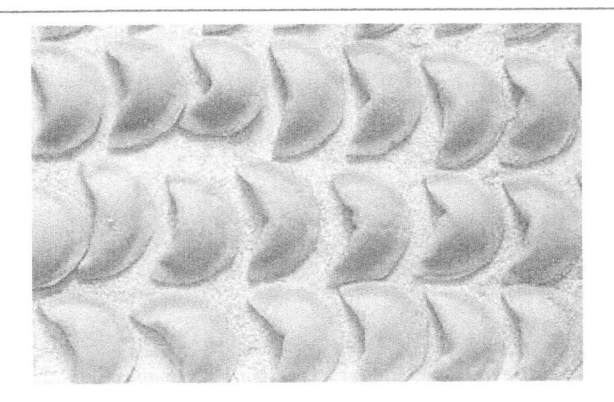

A pasta round folded in half to make a semicircle, commonly filled with a meat-and-grana-cheese filling.

CADUNSEI

Round dough disks folded in half, commonly stuffed with chicken giblets and herbs.

CANNELLONI

Sheets of pasta boiled and then rolled around filling— commonly meat, fish, or cheese—and then baked.

CAPPELLACCI

Shaped like a conical hat, these are made by first cutting dough into squares and then folding the dough square into a triangle, with the fulling in the core, pinching the two ends together, and then folding down the two corners sticking up. It can be filled with vegetables, such as squash, or meat-and-cheese fillings.

CAPPELLETTI

Small hat-shaped pasta made by folding a circular disk of pasta dough in half, bringing the two corners together to meet, and pinching them securely. Filler with a mixed meat filling or a cheese filling, and commonly cooked in broth.

CARAMELLE

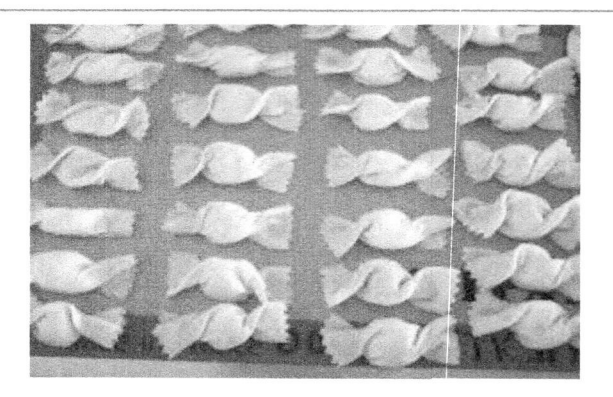

This pasta looks like a candy wrapper with twisted ends, and a filling in the center.

GNOCCHI

Gnocchi are a variety of pasta containing various thick, small, and soft dough dumplings that could be made from semolina, regular wheat flour, egg, cheese, potato, breadcrumbs, cornmeal or other ingredients like this, and can also include seasonings of herbs, vegetables, cocoa or prunes. The dough for gnocchi is commonly rolled out before it is cut into little pieces approximately the size of a wine cork. The little dumplings are then pressed using a fork or a cheese grater to make ridges that can hold sauce.

Dried Pasta

BUYING DRIED PASTA

There are a few things to keep in mind when buying dried pasta. It should be 100% semolina flour. The next thing to check is the protein content, and more protein content is always a higher quality dried pasta. A good pasta will have a protein content of approximately seventeen percent. The next thing to check is the finish. Rough finish is usually better than a smooth one. Also make sure the pasta is opaque, and not broken. Some of my favourite shapes are lengths, cranies, nooks, and ridges.

DRIED PASTA SHAPES

Dried pasta comes in so many shapes that If I try to write about all of them, I would have to write a whole book just to cover them all. Below is a picture that covers a few of the most common shapes popular all over the world.

PENNE	ORECCHIETTE	CONCHIGLIE	BUCATINI	RUOTE	PIPPE DOPPIA	
CAVATAPPI	FUSILLI	FARFALLE	SPAGHETTI	PIPE RIGATE	AVEMARIE	
MACARONI	RIGATONI	LASAGNE	RICCIOLI	PIPETTE RIGATE	GARGANELLI	
CANNELLONI	PAPPARDELLE	RAVIOLI	GNOCCHI	CRESTE DI GALLO	TAGLIATELLE CORTE	
STELLE	FIOCCHI RIGATI	RICCOLI	TORTIGLIONI	GEMELLI	FUSILLI	

Egg Pasta

Egg pasta can be both dry, or fresh. Depending on the kind of pasta, its shape too can vary. If it is dry, it can be of pretty much any shape shown in the dry pasta section, and if its fresh, it can have pretty much every fresh pasta shape we have seen.

Making egg pasta is quite fun, and here in Italy, we seldom buy this from a store. The number of eggs you use is up to your preference and taste. The texture of a good egg pasta is silky smooth.

Preparing, Saucing, and Serving Pasta

COOKING PASTA

If you can, season the pasta water using sea salt. Oil should never be poured into the cooking water as it covers the pasta and turns the texture slippery, so the sauce won't stick as intended to the pasta.

However, this is not hold true for a wide fresh pasta like lasagna, and you might need to use some oil to cook it so it does not stick together, and the lasagna will have time to absorb sauce while it bakes.

The best way to tell if a pasta is done cooking is to just cut out a tiny strand and eat it. If the texture has reached your desired level, turn off the heat. Once the pasta is done cooking, drin instantly, shaking off all the surplus water. Pasta should never be washed, unless you are making cold pasta dishes or baked pasta dishes such as lasagna or manicotti. Always sauce the pasta instantly, while it is still hot. After you have drained the pasta, put it back into the cooking pot, instantly put in a few tablespoons of sauce, and toss, or put drained pasta into a frying pan with sauce and toss well to dress the pasta.

USING PASTA WATER IN YOUR SAUCE

When cooking frying pan-sautéed pastas, it is essential to use the water in which the pasta was cooked again for the sauce-making stage and finishing the dish. After cooking all your seasonings and sauce ingredients, pour in water from the pasta pot as a medium to extract and blend their flavors. There is no need to put in stock, wine, or butter. In a big frying pan, the water will vaporize at a fast rate, so maintain the moisture using more pasta water as required. If your sauce is done but must wait some time for the pasta to cook, it may thicken, so put in pasta-cooking water. If there is to little sauce to completely coat the pasta when you're tossing it in the frying pan, put in some pasta water. In a nutshell, never drain pasta-cooking water into the sink.

MARINARA AND TOMATO SAUCE

Marinara sauce is quick and easy to make, seasoned only with garlic, crushed red pepper, and basil. I like to make it with San Marzano or plum tomatoes, crudely crushed manually or passed through a food mill. Marinara can be a little lumpy; the texture of the finished sauce is reasonably loose, and tastes like fresh tomatoes.

You have to work a little harder on the tomato sauce, beginning with pureed tomatoes seasoned with onion, carrot, celery, and bay leaf, and allowed to simmer until it becomes thick and rich in flavor. You can add a piece of fresh pork meat for additional flavor if you wish. It has a sweeter and more complex flavour.

HOW MUCH SAUCE DOES YOUR PASTA NEED?

It is important to have the right proportion of sauce and pasta, and at the end of the day the right proportion is one that tastes best for you. If you're a beginner and don't know what proportion to start with, just try to achieve a mixture where pasta glides in the sauce, and doesn't drown in it. When you're done eating the pasta, there should be negligible sauce left at the bottom of the bowl.

SERVING PASTA

Pasta is meant to be served fresh, immediately after it is cooked. It is most commonly served in heated bowls and heated plates. It is also a common practice for Italian families to bring the utensil in which the pasta is cooked right to the dining table, and everyone can help themselves to what they need. Always serve pasta with a bowl of freshly grated cheese if possible.

LEFTOVER PASTA

Although it is best enjoyed fresh, you can reheat pasta and enjoy it the next day too. One day old pasta tastes quite different from fresh pasta as it has had more time to absorb the sauces. Some people actually prefer a day old pasta to fresh pasta. So, feel free to make more pasta than you can handle, and enjoy it the next day too!

Rice, Seeds, Grains, and Bread

Italy has multiple staples when it comes to rice, seeds, grains, and bread. Some of the most important ingredients in this category are:

BARLEY

A delicious nutlike flavor and an appealing chewy, pastalike consistency is a versatile ingredient in Italian dishes, and used in a wide variety of ways.

BREAD

Bread is a part of pretty much every table set with an Italian course.

FARRO

A classic Italian staple, if you haven't tried this grain yet, now is the time to do so!

FETTE BISCOTTATE

These delicious crackers are enjoyed for breakfast all over Italy!

PINE NUTS

Pinoli nuts are an Italian staple used in fish and vegetable preparations. They should be stored in airtight plastic bags in the refrigerator for maximum three months.

POLENTA

Polenta is enjoyed in so many ways here in Italy that I could write a whole book about it. Add this gem of an ingredient to your pantry if you're serious about cooking authentic Italian dishes on a regular basis.

RICE, ITALIAN VARIETIES

Rice is a staple in all of the world. It is inexpensive, easy to cook, and tastes great with pretty much everything. A few of the popular Italian rice varieties are: Arborio, Carnaroli, and Vialone Nano. You can easily find these varieties in a store near you, or online on amazon.

WHEAT BERRIES

The term "wheat berry" refers to the complete wheat kernel, except the hull. Wheat berries are normally tan to reddish brown in color and can be bought either hard, when they are packaged dried, or tender and usually partially cooked, when they are packed in a can as a processed grain.

Fish and Seafood

Italy is a Mediterranean country, and the Mediterranean sea has always been bountiful. Although not as rich today due to over-fishing as it was a few decades back, the sea is still bountiful and provides sustenance to millions. Here are a few Italian favorites from the sea:

- Anchovies
- Baccalà
- Calamari (squid)
- Clams
- Lobster
- Monkfish—a great cooking fish
- Octopus

- Razor clams
- Scallops
- Scungilli
- Shrimp
- Skate
- Soft-shell crab
- Swordfish
- Tuna
- Whole individual portion fish: snapper, branzino, striped bass, black bass, etc.

Meat

Italy has some Insanely delicious meaty delicacies. The most popular meat varieties in Italy are:

- Beef
- Boar meat
- Chicken
- Duck and quail
- Eggs
- Lamb
- Offal
- Pork
- Prosciutto
- Rabbit
- Speck

- Squab and pheasant
- Veal
- Venison

Wine, Beer, and Other Drinks

Italy is well known for wine making and beer brewing all over the world. Most Italian dishes are best enjoyed with a glass of wine or beer on the side. In moderation, wine is an important component of a healthy Italian diet.

Wine

Not all wines are created equal. Know what you need to make your Italian course truly authentic.

READING ITALIAN WINE LABELS

Ever seen DOC and DOCG written on Italian wine labels? If you're looking for an authentic Italian wine, make sure you look for these.

DOC indicates wine that is "Vino a Denominazione di Origine Controllata," which means the wine wines are produced in well-defined regions in accordance with very particular rules that were put in place to preserve traditional wine-making practices in that region.

"Vino a Denominazione di Origine Controllata e Garantita," or DOCG, is comparatively even more strict certification system that represents only a handful of Italian wines. DOCG wines must pass a taste test, and growers are not allowed to produce more than a pre-defined amount of wine.

There are other wines out there that are brilliant, and carry none of these certifications. Feel free to explore the market and try new things! If you're a beginner and don't know what to get, these labels will help.

PAIRING FOOD AND WINE

Don't burn your brain cells figuring out what wine will go well with the course you are planning. If in doubt, just go grab any Italian wine with a certification mentioned above, and you should have a good time. Make sure you try a different wine the next time, and a different wine the next, until you know what works for you, and what wine you like best.

COOKING WITH WINE

If you want to go for authenticity, cook using a wine you would normally drink. Cooking wines are cheap, and contain added salt and seasonings that can alter the flavour of the final dish. White wine or red wine? Both do the job. Try them both once, and stick with the one you like better for a particular recipe.

BEER

There is nothing like cracking open a cold one on a hot day. Italians sure don't miss out on this pleasure, and beer is one of the most popular drinks all over Italy.

COOKING WITH BEER

Just like wine, beer is also used to cook a wide variety of recipes. Just go ahead and use a quality beer you love to drink, and you will be fine.

Coffee

Most of the Italian coffee recipes you enjoy in the coffee shop near you are of Italian origin. It goes without saying that coffee is an integral part of Italian cuisine.

Basic Italian Cooking Techniques

General Tips

Before we dive into the recipes, I would like to talk about a few cooking basics that you probably already know.

ADJUST SEASONING WHILE YOU COOK

This book does provide some idea about the amount of seasoning that will work for a particular recipe, but if you're not sure, always add less seasoning that you think is right for you. It is easy to add more later, but impossible to extract the seasoning once combined.

Taste the recipe while it is cooking, and adjust the seasoning accordingly.

SHOPPING FOR FOOD

Buy local, buy fresh, buy ingredients that are in season. Find a nice farmer's market close to you, and even if they cost a little more, I say it is totally worth it.

STORING FOOD

Different foods have different ideal storage methods. If you're unsure about how a particular ingredient or dish should be stored, google is your friend.

KEEP YOUR PANTRY READY

We have already talked about Italian staples in detail in previous sections. Once you start making the recipes, you will have an even better idea of what you will need on a regular basis. Keep your pantry stocked with these items so that you can always cook an Italian dish when you're in the mood for it, without heading out to a nearby store for every little ingredient you're missing.

FOOD IS WASTE

We Italians frown upon food wastage, and you should too. It is ok to have leftovers, as long as they get eaten the next day, and don't have to be thrown into the dustbin. If there are some leftovers you don't know how store, just google it. Be creative in re-using the leftovers, and save money, and the planet.

SAFETY

Things coming out of the oven are hot, so it is a good idea to have mitts. Also be careful while chopping stuff up, especially if you're new to chopping. If you're a news with a knife, take things slow. You'll get better with time, trust me.

BUTTER AND OIL

Oils that don't smoke easily are the best. These oils are usually costlier, but much better for health. So, oils with a high smoking temperature like canola oil are the best for frying, while vegetable oils are moderate, and butter is the worst.

SERVING

Cooking a delicious meal is important, but making the meal look delicious is important too, especially if you're serving to guests. Italian dishes look great over white plates, with a bit of garnish.

Tools

Italian cooking is quite standard, and you will probably already have most of the tools this book calls for. You might not have some of the things mentioned below, and you don't need to invest in these just yet. For example, you can easily do without the pasta-maker Chitarra, but if you want to go all in with authentic Italian cooking, you might want to invest in one.

CHITARRA FOR MACCHERONI

This pasta maker looks like a musical instrument, and if you want to make authentic fresh pasta, this tool will come in handy. It will take some space in your kitchen, so don't invest in one until you're serious about pasta.

KNIVES

Italian food requires you to chop stuff up, and you will need knives to do that.

MANDOLINE SLICER

A handy tool that makes chopping some vegetables and fruits an absolute breeze.

MORTAR AND PESTLE

You will be making a lot of sauces and crushing a lot of ingredients together. A mortar and pestle will come in handy.

PIZZA STONE

This is a dedicated tablet for making pizzas. If you don't have one, you can do the job using a baking sheet on any surface, or a cast-iron frying pan.

POTATO RICER

Italians love Gnocchi dough, and this tool makes the job of making it a breeze!

Cooking Methods

If you've been cooking for a while, you've probably mastered all the techniques mentioned below already. If not, you will need a bit of practice and you'll be fine.

BAKING

Dry heating for a long duration. Usually done using an oven. Breads, cakes, cookies, etc. all require baking.

BRAISING

This cooking method makes use of both moist and dry heat. Most braises follow the same basic steps. To start, the food is seared at a high temperature to caramelize its surface and boost its flavor. Next, flavorful liquids, such as wine, stock, beer, vinegar, and juice, as well as herbs and spices, are poured into the pot, the pot is covered to allow the food to incorporate the flavours and get enhanced.

BROILING

A simple cooking method where food is exposed to direct heat. The heat source could be a gas flame, electric coil, live coals, etc.

BRINING

The food is immersed in a brine solution for sex to twelve hours before cooking.

FRYING

One of the most cooking methods out there. Food is cooked completely immersed in a fat on in a deep pan.

GRILLING

Food is exposed to intense direct heat. Usually the food is seasoned before it is grilled.

MARINATING

Food is immersed in a solution, usually acidic for a long period of time before it is cooked. Marinating enhances the flavour of the food.

POACHING

The process of slowly simmering food in liquids such as milk, stock, wine, tomato sauce, vegetable sauce, or juices.

ROASTING

Roasting means searing the food with dry heat, whether an open flame, a wood-burning oven, or a gas or electric oven.

SAUTÉING

Food is heated in presence of a small amount of fat on a flat frying pan.

STEAMING

Water is boiled, and the steam created is used to cook the food. The benefit of steaming is that the food doesn't most of its nutrients and flavour to the water as it does in case of boiling.

MEASUREMENTS FOR NON-US COOKS

American cooks use standard containers, the 8-ounce cup and a tablespoon that takes exactly 16 level fillings to fill that cup level. Measuring by cup makes it very difficult to give weight equivalents, as the density plays an important role when it comes to weight. The easiest way therefore to deal with cup measurements in recipes is to take the amount by volume rather than by weight. Thus, the equation reads:

1 cup = 240ml = 8 fluid Ounces

½ cup = 120ml = 4 fluid ounces

It is possible to buy a set of American cup measures in major stores around the world.

In the States, butter is sometimes measured in sticks. One stick is the equivalent of 8 tablespoons. One tablespoon of butter is therefore the equivalent to ½ ounce/15 grams.

Liquid Measures

1 Teaspoon= 5 Millilitres

1 Tablespoon = 14 millilitres

2 Tablespoons= 1 Fluid Ounce

Solid Measures

1 Ounce= 28 Grams

16 Ounces= 1 Pound

Appetizers

Artichoke and Mint Frittata	65
Baked Clams Oreganata	66
Baked Eggplant and Eggs	67
Baked Eggs With White Truffles	69
Baked Mushroom Crostini	71
Calf's Brain In A Lemon Sauce	72
Celery Stalks Stuffed With Gorgonzola and Apples	74
Cheese Baked In A Crust	75
Chicken Liver Crostini	76
Clams Casino	77
Egg-Battered Zucchini Roll-Ups	79
Eggplant Rollatini	81
Eggs Poached In Tomato Sauce	83
Eggs Scrambled In Tomato Sauce	85
Fava and Sesame Dip	86
Frico With Montasio Cheese and Apples	87
Frico With Montasio Cheese and Potatoes	89
Lentil Crostini	91
Lettuce and Bread Quiches	92
Mussels In Spicy Tomato Sauce	94
Prosciutto and Fig Bruschetta	96
Provolone Turnovers	97
Rice and Zucchini Crostata	99
Rice Balls	102
Ricotta Frittata	104
Roasted Pepper Rolls Stuffed With Tuna	105
Rosemary and Lemon Focaccia	107
Sausage Crostini	112
Sausage, Bread, and Pepper Frittata	113
Scrambled Eggs and Asparagus	115
Steamed Mussels In Savory Wine Sauce	115
Stuffed Artichokes	117
Stuffed Mushrooms	119
Stuffed Olives Ascolane	121

Stuffed Zucchini Blossoms 123
Swiss Chard and Potato Crostata 125
Swordfish-Stuffed Peppers 127
Tomato Fritters 129
Whipped Salt Cod Spread 130
Zucchini Fritters 132

We Italians love to start a course with appetizers. In this section, we will look at some of the most popular appetizers in Italy!

Figure 1: Baked Clams Oreganata

Artichoke and Mint Frittata

Frittata di Carciofi con Menta (Italian Name of the Recipe)

Yield: Servings 4 To 6

Ingredients:

- ¼ cup extra-virgin olive oil
- 8 small artichokes, trimmed and cleaned, chokes removed, halved and sliced ¼ inch thick
- 1¼ teaspoons kosher salt
- 1 bunch scallions, trimmed and cut into ½-inch pieces
- 8 big eggs
- 2 tablespoons chopped fresh mint

Directions:

1. Heat a medium (10-inch) nonstick frying pan on moderate heat. Put in the oil. When the oil is hot, put in the artichokes and 1 teaspoon of the salt. Toss to coat the artichokes in the oil, then cover and cook until soft, stirring a couple of times, approximately fifteen minutes.
2. Uncover, put in the scallions, and cook until wilted, approximately three to four minutes more. In the meantime, in a large container, beat the eggs with the rest of the ¼ teaspoon salt and the mint. Pour the eggs into the frying pan and cover. Decrease the heat to

moderate low, and cook until just set, approximately ten minutes.
3. Invert onto a plate, and slide back into the frying pan to brown the other side, approximately five minutes more. Slide onto a cutting board, and let cool at least five minutes before cutting into wedges to serve. Can be served warm or at room temperature.

Baked Clams Oreganata

Vongole Ripiene al Forno (Italian Name of the Recipe)

Yield: Servings 6

Ingredients:

- ¼ cup finely chopped fresh Italian parsley
- ½ cup dry white wine
- ½ cup finely chopped red bell pepper
- ½ teaspoon kosher salt
- 1 teaspoon dried oregano, preferably Sicilian on the branch
- 1½ cups fine dried bread crumbs
- 36 littleneck clams, shucked, juices reserved
- 6 tablespoons extra-virgin olive oil
- Lemon wedges, for serving (not necessary)

Directions:

1. Preheat your oven to 425 degrees. As you shuck the clams, set them aside and reserve and strain their juices. Coarsely cut the shucked clams, and put in a large container. Put in the bread crumbs, bell pepper, 2 tablespoons parsley, the oregano, and salt. Sprinkle with 2 tablespoons olive oil, and toss using a fork to combine.
2. Stuff the clamshells with the filling, and place on a rimmed baking sheet; pour any extra juice, along with the white wine, into the bottom of the pan. Sprinkle the clams with 3 tablespoons olive oil, and sprinkle the rest of the tablespoon oil and rest of the 2 tablespoons chopped parsley into the bottom of the pan. Bake until the clam stuffing is browned and crunchy, approximately fifteen minutes. To serve: set the clams on a plate with rest of the sauce and fresh lemon wedges for squeezing (if using).

Baked Eggplant and Eggs

Melanzane e Uova al Forno (Italian Name of the Recipe)

Yield: Servings 6

Ingredients:

- ¼ teaspoon crushed red pepper flakes
- 1 cup freshly grated Grana Padano
- 1 teaspoon dried oregano, preferably Sicilian on the branch

- 1 teaspoon kosher salt, plus more for salting the eggplant
- 2 sprigs fresh basil, plus 6 big leaves
- 3 garlic cloves, sliced
- 3 Italian eggplants (approximately 1¼ pounds total)
- 6 big eggs
- 6 tablespoons extra-virgin olive oil, plus more for brushing the gratin dishes
- All-purpose flour, for dredging
- One 28-ounce can Italian plum tomatoes, preferably San Marzano, crushed by hand

Directions:

1. With a vegetable peeler, peel strips along the length down the eggplant, leaving alternate stripes of peel. Cut off stems, and slice eggplant along the length into ¼-inch-thick slices. Line a big colander with the eggplant, overlapping if necessary; salt liberally on both sides, and allow to drain in the sink for half an hour. Rinse, drain, and dry the eggplant well.
2. Preheat your oven to 350 degrees. In the meantime, to a big frying pan on moderate to high heat, put in 3 tablespoons of the olive oil. When the oil is hot, put in the garlic. Let the garlic sizzle until golden, approximately 1 minute, then pour in the tomatoes. Wash the tomato can with 1 cup water, and put in that too. Season with 1 teaspoon kosher salt and the crushed red pepper flakes.

Stick the basil sprigs in the sauce. Let the sauce simmer until a little thickened, approximately fifteen minutes. Remove basil sprigs.
3. Spread the flour on a plate. Lightly dredge the dried eggplant in flour, tapping off the surplus. Heat the rest of the 3 tablespoons olive oil in a big frying pan on moderate to high heat. When the oil is hot, brown the eggplant in batches, approximately 2 minutes per side. Take the slices as they brown, and drain on a paper-towel-lined sheet pan.
4. Once the sauce and eggplant are ready, brush six individual gratin dishes with olive oil. Spread a scant ¼ cup of sauce in the bottom of each dish. Fold the eggplant slices to line and fit the gratin dishes in a uniform layer. Spread another scant ¼ cup of sauce over the eggplant. Drizzle sauce with approximately ¾ cup cheese. Lay a basil leaf over the cheese, and crack an egg into each dish. Drizzle with the rest of the grated cheese and the dried oregano.
5. Put dishes on a baking sheet, and cover with foil. Bake until sauce is bubbly, approximately fifteen minutes. Uncover, and bake until cheese is browned and eggs are done to your preference, approximately five minutes more for almost set yolks.

Baked Eggs With White Truffles

Uova con Tartufo Bianco (Italian Name of the Recipe)

Yield: Servings 6

Ingredients:

- 1 white truffle about the size of a walnut
- 4 tablespoons unsalted butter, softened
- 6 big eggs
- 6 tablespoons heavy cream
- 6 tablespoons milk
- Kosher salt and freshly ground black pepper
- Six ½-inch-thick slices country bread

Directions:

1. Preheat your oven to 325 degrees. Clean the white truffle (or truffles, if you're feeling especially extravagant) of all loose soil with a vegetable brush, and tenderly remove any dirt that is embedded in the edges using a paring knife.
2. Chop the bread into sticks about the width of your finger, and toast in the oven on a sheet pan until crunchy, approximately ten minutes. Allow to cool.
3. Brush six ramekins (3 inches in diameter) with 1 tablespoon of the softened butter. Pour 1 tablespoon milk and 1 tablespoon heavy cream into each of the ramekins. Chop the rest of the 3 tablespoons butter into six pieces, and put in a piece to each ramekin. Cautiously break an egg into each ramekin, taking care not to break

the yolk. Sprinkle with salt and pepper. Use a truffle slicer or Microplane grater to shave the rough edges on the outside of the truffle over the eggs, saving for later the white inside of the truffle to put in after baking.
4. Put the ramekins in a deep baking pan, and put in hot water to come halfway up the sides. Bake approximately 10 to twelve minutes for cooked whites with still-runny yolks. Transfer ramekins to plates, and shave over the eggs the rest of the truffle. Serve with the toast sticks for dipping.

Baked Mushroom Crostini

Crostini di Funghi al Forno (Italian Name of the Recipe)

Yield: Servings 4

Ingredients:

- ¼ cup extra-virgin olive oil
- ½ cup freshly grated Grana Padano
- ½ teaspoon kosher salt
- 1 cup grated Italian Fontina
- 1 pound mixed fresh mushrooms, sliced (cremini, button, shiitake, oyster, chanterelle)
- 2 tablespoons chopped fresh Italian parsley
- 3 garlic cloves, crushed and peeled
- 4 fresh sage leaves, chopped
- 8 slices country bread, very lightly toasted

Directions:

1. Preheat your oven to 400 degrees. To a big frying pan on moderate to high heat, put in 2 tablespoons of the olive oil. When the oil is hot, put in the garlic cloves. Once the garlic is sizzling, put in the mushrooms and sage, and cook, without stirring, until browned on one side, approximately two to three minutes. Stir, and brown the other side. Season with the salt, cover, and cook until soft, approximately five minutes. Uncover, remove the garlic, mix in the parsley, and set aside.
2. On a baking sheet, brush the lightly toasted bread on both sides with the rest of the 2 tablespoons olive oil. In a moderate-sized container, toss together the grated cheeses. Stir half of the cheese mixture into the mushrooms.
3. Spread the mushroom mixture on the toasts, and drizzle with the rest of the grated-cheese mixture. Bake until the tops are browned and the cheese is bubbly, approximately ten to twelve minutes. Serve hot.

Calf's Brain In A Lemon Sauce

Cervella di Vitello al Limone (Italian Name of the Recipe)

Yield: Servings 4 To 6

Ingredients:

- ½ cup white wine vinegar
- ½ teaspoon kosher salt, plus more for the pot
- 1 pound calf's brain
- 2 tablespoons chopped fresh Italian parsley
- 2 tablespoons drained tiny capers in brine
- 6 tablespoons extra-virgin olive oil
- 8 cups mixed greens
- Freshly ground black pepper
- Juice of 1 lemon, freshly squeezed

Directions:

1. Trim the brain of all surface membranes and blood lines, or make the butcher do this while purchasing. In a big glass or ceramic container, combine 1 quart water and the vinegar. Put in the brain, and weight it with a plate to keep it submerged. Place in your fridge 2 hours.
2. Bring a big pot of salted water to its boiling point. Drain and wash the brain well. Put in the brain to the boiling water, and simmer until thoroughly cooked, approximately fifteen minutes. Drain, rinse, and pat dry. Salt lightly. Allow to cool to room temperature, then place in your fridge until completely chilled, minimum 2 hours.
3. Trim away any stray membranes, and thinly slice the brain. Position the brains on a bed of the greens on chilled serving plates. In a moderate-sized container, whisk together the olive oil and lemon juice. Whisk in the

rest of the salt and season with pepper. Whisk in the parsley and capers. Sprinkle the dressing over the plated brains and greens, and serve instantly.

Celery Stalks Stuffed With Gorgonzola and Apples

Coste di Sedano Farcite al Gorgonzola e Mele (Italian Name of the Recipe)

Yield: Servings 4 To 6

Ingredients:

- ½ cup inner celery leaves, for garnish
- ½ Granny Smith apple, with skin, finely diced
- ¾ cup mascarpone, at room temperature
- 4 ounces Gorgonzola Dolce, at room temperature
- 6 inner celery stalks, trimmed and cut into 3 pieces each

Directions:

1. In a moderate-sized container, purée together the Gorgonzola and mascarpone until the desired smoothness is achieved. Mix in the diced apple, and mix thoroughly.
2. With a teaspoon, stuff the mixture into the celery stalks. Chill for about 1 hour before you serve, and serve garnished with the celery leaves.

Cheese Baked In A Crust

Formaggio in Crosta (Italian Name of the Recipe)

Yield: Servings 6

Ingredients:

- 1 big egg, beaten
- 1 sheet frozen puff pastry, thawed in accordance with package directions
- 12 cups mixed baby greens
- 2 tablespoons heavy cream
- 4 ounces Gorgonzola, at room temperature, or 6 ounces Taleggio (because rind will be removed)
- Kosher salt and freshly ground black pepper
- Red wine vinegar and extra-virgin olive oil, for dressing the greens

Directions:

1. Preheat your oven to 425 degrees. Crumble the Gorgonzola into a moderate-sized container, and purée with the cream. Lightly mould into six balls; they should just hold together, not be compacted. Chill while you roll the pastry.
2. On a floured work surface, roll out the pastry sheet to a little thicker than ⅛ inch. Using a bowl with a 5-inch diameter as your reference, cut six rounds from the pastry.

3. Put the rounds on a parchment-lined baking sheet, and chill in your fridge for about ten minutes.
4. Take the rounds out of the fridge, and place a cheese ball in the center of each. Brush the edges with the egg, and fold each into a half-moon. Push or crimp using a fork to secure. Brush the tops with more egg. Bake until puffed, browned, and crisp, approximately twelve minutes. Allow to cool ten minutes before you serve. Before you serve, toss the greens lightly with vinegar and olive oil in a large container, and sprinkle with salt and pepper. Serve the baked cheese puffs on plates with a side of dressed greens.

Chicken Liver Crostini

Crostini di Fegatini di Pollo (Italian Name of the Recipe)

Makes About 12 Crostini, Serving 6

Ingredients:

- ¼ teaspoon kosher salt
- ½ cup dry Marsala
- 1 cup finely chopped shallots
- 12 ounces chicken livers, trimmed of fat and membranes, halved
- 12 slices Italian baguette, grilled or toasted
- 2 tablespoons unsalted butter
- 3 tablespoons drained tiny capers in brine

- 3 tablespoons extra-virgin olive oil
- 6 fresh sage leaves, chopped

Directions:

1. To a big frying pan over low heat, put in the olive oil and the shallots, and cook, stirring once in a while, until the shallots become tender but not browned, approximately five minutes.
2. Increase heat to moderate high, and put in the capers and sage. Once they begin sizzling, put in the chicken livers. Toss and cook until browned, approximately three to four minutes; then put in the Marsala. Season with the salt, and cook until the Marsala is reduced by half, approximately three to four minutes. Whisk in the butter, turn off the heat, and let cool.
3. When the chicken livers have cooled, purée the mixture in a food processor until almost smooth (a few chunks are okay). Spread on the grilled or toasted bread, before you serve.

Clams Casino

Vongole al Forno con Pancetta (Italian Name of the Recipe)

Yield: Servings 6 As An Appetizer

Ingredients:

- 2 red or yellow bell peppers, roasted, peeled, and cut into 1-inch squares
- 3 tablespoons chopped fresh Italian parsley
- 3 tablespoons unsalted butter
- 36 littleneck clams on the half-shell
- 6 ounces thinly sliced bacon, cut into 1-inch squares
- Dry white wine, as needed

Directions:

1. Get the 36 clams shucked clams by a nearby seafood shop, or shuck them yourself. (Lots of video tutorials on YouTube) Save the clams and their juices for later.
2. Preheat your oven to 450 degrees. Put clams on a rimmed baking sheet in one even layer. Top each clam in the shell with a pepper square and a bacon square (bacon on top). Top with a dab of butter, using all 3 tablespoons uniformly. Drizzle with chopped parsley.
3. Pour the reserved shucking juices into a 2-cup measure. Put in enough white wine to make 1½ cups liquid, and pour into the bottom of the baking sheet. Bake the clams, uncovered, until the bacon is crunchy and the clams are cooked all the way through, approximately twenty to twenty-five minutes. Serve on a platter, sprinkled with the baking juices.

Egg-Battered Zucchini Roll-Ups

Involtini di Zucchine Fritte (Italian Name of the Recipe)

Yield: Servings 10 As An Hors D'oeuvre Or 6 As A Side Dish

Ingredients:

- ¾ teaspoon salt
- 1 or 2 tablespoons drained tiny capers in brine
- 2 cups all-purpose flour, for dredging
- 2 pounds (5 or 6) small zucchini
- 5 big eggs
- Canola or vegetable oil, for frying (2 cups or more, depending on frying pan size)
- Freshly ground black pepper to taste
- Juice of ½ lemon, freshly squeezed

Directions:

1. Wash and dry the zucchini, and trim off the stem and blossom ends. With a shafp knife, slice the squash along the length into strips about ⅛ inch thick, flexible but not paper-thin. (You should get around five or from each small zucchini.)
2. Put the flour into a wide container or shallow dish. Beat the eggs thoroughly in a different wide container, mixing in ½ teaspoon of the salt and some grinds of pepper. Set a wide colander on a plate, to drain the battered strips

before frying. Tumble five or six zucchini strips at a time in the flour, coating them thoroughly on both sides.

3. Shake off the loose flour, and slide the strips into the beaten eggs. Turn and separate the strips using a fork so they're coated with batter; pick them up one by one, allowing the surplus egg to drip back into the container; lay the strips in the colander. Dredge and batter all the zucchini strips this way, and allow them to drain. Return the egg drippings collected under the colander to the batter, if more is required.
4. Pour an inch of oil into a deep frying pan, and set it on moderate to high heat. Coat a baking sheet or big platter with paper towels. When the oil is very hot but not smoking, test it by dropping in half a strip of battered zucchini. It should sizzle energetically and start to crisp around the edges, but not smoke or darken.
5. Fry the zucchini strips in batches, and when they are golden on both sides, remove them and set on the paper towels to drain, approximately 4 to five minutes per batch. Drizzle with rest of the salt.
6. To form the roll-ups: Put a fried strip on your worktable, with the wider end facing you. Put three or four capers on that end, then vertically roll the strip firmly, enclosing the capers in the center. Weave a toothpick all the way through the roll-up, so it stays secure. Roll up all the strips. Just before you serve, stand the roll-ups on end and squeeze drops of lemon juice all over the spiral tops. Position them on a serving platter.

Eggplant Rollatini

Involtini di Melanzane (Italian Name of the Recipe)

Yield: Servings 6 As A Main Course Or 12 As A First Course Or Buffet Serving

Ingredients:

- ½ cup extra-virgin olive oil, or as needed
- ½ cup vegetable oil, or as needed
- 1 cup freshly grated Grana Padano
- 1½ pounds fresh ricotta, or 3 cups whole-milk ricotta
- 2 medium eggplants (about 2 pounds total)
- 3 big eggs
- 3 cups Tomato Sauce
- 3 tablespoons chopped fresh Italian parsley
- 8 fresh basil leaves
- 8 ounces fresh mozzarella, cut into ¼-by-¼-inch sticks
- All-purpose flour
- Freshly ground black pepper
- Kosher salt

Directions:

1. Spoon the ricotta into a big fine-mesh sieve, or a colander lined with a twofold thickness of cheesecloth. Set the sieve over a container, and cover the ricotta well using plastic wrap. Drain the ricotta in your fridge

minimum overnight, or maximum one day. Discard the liquid in the bottom of the container.

2. Preheat your oven to 375 degrees. Warm the tomato sauce in a small deep cooking pan. Trim the stems and ends from the eggplants. Remove alternating strips of peel approximately 1 inch wide from the eggplants, leaving about half the peel undamaged. Chop the eggplants along the length into ¼-inch-thick slices, and place them in a colander. Drizzle liberally with the kosher salt, tossing to expose all slices, and allow to drain for an hour. Wash the eggplant under cool running water, drain well, and pat dry.

3. Pour ½ cup each of the olive and vegetable oils into a medium frying pan on moderate to high heat. While the oil heats, whisk two of the eggs and 1 teaspoon salt together in a wide, shallow container. Spread approximately 1 cup flour in a different wide, shallow container. Dredge the eggplant slices in flour, shaking off the surplus. Immerse the floured eggplant into the egg mixture, turning well to coat both sides uniformly. Let surplus egg drip back into the container.

4. When a corner of a coated eggplant slice gives off a lively sizzle when dipped into the hot oil, the oil is ready for frying. Put in as many of the coated eggplant slices as fit without touching, and cook, flipping over once, until golden on both sides, approximately 4 minutes. Take the eggplant to a sheet pan lined with paper towels and repeat with the rest of the eggplant slices. Regulate the

heat as the eggplant cooks, to stop the egg coating from cooking too fast or overbrowning or the oil temperature from plummeting. Put in oil to the pan as required during cooking to keep the level nearly the same. Let the new oil heat before you put in more eggplant slices.

5. Mix the drained ricotta, ⅔ cup of the grated cheese, and the parsley together in a mixing bowl. Taste, and sprinkle with salt and pepper. Beat the rest of the egg and stir it into the ricotta mixture. Pour 1 cup of the tomato sauce over the bottom of a 10-by-15-inch baking dish. Drizzle lightly with 2 tablespoons of the rest of the grated cheese.

6. Lay one of the fried eggplant slices in front of you, with the short end toward you. Spoon about 2 tablespoons of the ricotta filling over the thin end of the slice, and top it with a mozzarella stick. Roll, and place, seam side down, in the prepared baking dish. Repeat with the rest of the eggplant slices and filling, placing the rolls side by side.

7. Ladle the rest of the tomato sauce over the eggplant rolls to coat them uniformly. Drizzle the rest of the grated cheese over the top of the eggplant, and tear the basil leaves over the cheese. Cover the dish loosely with foil, and bake until bubbling and the filling is thoroughly heated, approximately half an hour. Allow to rest ten minutes before you serve.

Eggs Poached In Tomato Sauce

Uova Affogate in Salsa di Pomodoro (Italian Name of the Recipe)

Yield: Servings 6

Ingredients:

- ¼ teaspoon crushed red pepper flakes
- ½ teaspoon dried oregano, preferably Sicilian on the branch
- ¾ teaspoon kosher salt
- 4 garlic cloves, thinly sliced
- 5 tablespoons extra-virgin olive oil
- 6 big eggs
- 6 slices grilled country bread, for serving
- One 28-ounce can Italian plum tomatoes, preferably San Marzano, passed through a food mill

Directions:

1. To a big frying pan on moderate heat, put in the olive oil. When the oil is hot, put in the garlic. Once the garlic is sizzling, in about one minute, put in the red pepper flakes. Pour in the tomatoes and 1 cup water used to wash out the tomato can. Bring to a simmer. Season with ½ teaspoon salt and dried oregano. Simmer until it becomes thick, approximately twenty minutes. The sauce is adequately thickened when you can see the bottom of the frying pan as you drag a wooden spoon on the base of the frying pan.

2. Break one egg into a ramekin or small container. Lightly slide the egg into the simmering sauce. Repeat with the rest of the eggs, spacing them uniformly in the sauce. Season the eggs with the rest of the ¼ teaspoon salt. Baste the eggs with a little sauce, cover, and cook until done, approximately five minutes for set whites with still-runny yolks. Serve in shallow containers, with some sauce and grilled bread.

Eggs Scrambled In Tomato Sauce

Uova Strapazzate al Pomodoro (Italian Name of the Recipe)

Yield: Servings 6

Ingredients:

- ¼ cup fresh basil leaves, coarsely shredded
- ¼ cup freshly grated Grana Padano
- ¼ teaspoon crushed red pepper flakes
- ½ teaspoon dried oregano, preferably Sicilian on the branch
- ¾ teaspoon kosher salt
- 4 garlic cloves, thinly sliced
- 5 tablespoons extra-virgin olive oil
- 6 big eggs
- 6 slices grilled country bread, for serving

- One 28-ounce can Italian plum tomatoes, preferably San Marzano, passed through a food mill

Directions:

1. To a big frying pan on moderate heat, put in the olive oil. When the oil is hot, put in the garlic. Once the garlic is sizzling, in about one minute, put in the red pepper flakes. Pour in the tomatoes and 1 cup water used to wash out the tomato can. Bring to a simmer. Season with ½ teaspoon salt and dried oregano. Simmer until it becomes thick, approximately twenty minutes. The sauce is adequately thickened when you can see the bottom of the frying pan when you drag a wooden spoon through.
2. In a moderate-sized container, beat the eggs with the grated cheese and rest of the ¼ teaspoon salt. Whisk the eggs into the simmering sauce using a fork, stirring to make raggedy pieces or *stracciatella*, until eggs are cooked, approximately 3 minutes. Mix in the basil, and serve in shallow containers with the grilled bread.

Fava and Sesame Dip

Crema di Fave e Sesamo (Italian Name of the Recipe)

Yield: Servings 4 To 6

Ingredients:

- ¼ cup freshly squeezed lemon juice

- ½ cup sesame seeds, lightly toasted
- ⅔ cup extra-virgin olive oil
- ¾ teaspoon kosher salt, plus more for the pot
- 1 garlic clove, crushed and peeled
- 4 pounds fresh fava beans (3 to 3½ cups), shelled
- Flatbread or bread sticks, for serving

Directions:

1. Bring a big pot of salted water to its boiling point. Put in the shelled favas, and blanch until bright green and tender, approximately five to seven minutes, depending on their size. Cool in a container of ice water. Remove the skins and discard. You should have about 2 cups peeled favas.
2. Use a food processor to mix the favas, sesame seeds (reserving 1 tablespoon for garnish), lemon juice, garlic, and salt. With the machine running, put in the olive oil in a stream to make a thick, lumpy paste. With the machine still running, put in warm water, a few tablespoons at a time (up to ⅓ cup), to thin the dip to your preference. It must be about the consistency of hummus.
3. Move the dip to a serving container. Decorate using rest of the sesame seeds, and serve with flatbread or bread sticks for dipping.

Frico With Montasio Cheese and Apples

Frico con le Mele (Italian Name of the Recipe)

Yield: Servings 6

Ingredients:

- 1 tablespoon extra-virgin olive oil
- 2 small Golden Delicious or other firm apples (approximately 12 ounces)
- 8 ounces Montasio cheese, shredded

Directions:

1. Peel and core the apples, and slice into wedges about ½ inch thick. Heat the olive oil in a moderate-sized nonstick frying pan on moderate heat. Scatter the apple wedges in the pan, and toss to coat with oil. Cook and caramelize the apples for approximately eight minutes, tossing regularly, until tinged with brown and softened but not mushy. Scrape the caramelized apples onto a plate.
2. Drizzle half of the shredded Montasio in a uniform layer over the bottom of the frying pan. Return the apples to the pan, spreading them uniformly on top of the cheese, then drizzle the remainder of the shredded cheese over the apples.
3. Reduce the heat, and allow the frico to cook, uninterrupted, until the bottom is very brown and crisped, approximately ten minutes. If the cheese releases a lot of fat in the pan, blot it up with paper towels. Shake the pan to loosen the disk, put a big plate

on top, and invert, dropping the frico onto the plate, then slide it back into the frying pan, top side down. Cook until the second side is crisp and brown, approximately seven minutes more. Slide (or invert) the frico onto the plate, blot up oil, and slice into six wedges. Serve hot.

Frico With Montasio Cheese and Potatoes

Frico con Patate (Italian Name of the Recipe)

Yield: Servings 6

Ingredients:

- ¼ teaspoon kosher salt
- ½ cup thinly sliced scallions
- 1 medium baking potato (approximately eight ounces)
- 1 small onion, sliced
- 2 tablespoons extra-virgin olive oil
- 8 ounces Montasio cheese, shredded
- Freshly ground black pepper to taste

Directions:

1. Cook the potato in a pan of gently boiling water just until it is effortlessly pierced using a sharp knife all the way through, but still undamaged and not mushy. Drain and cool the potato, remove the skin, and cut it into neat ¼-inch-thick rounds.

2. Pour the olive oil into a moderate-sized nonstick frying pan, set on moderate heat, and scatter in the sliced onion and scallions. Cook for one minute, then scatter the potato rounds in the pan. Lightly toss the potatoes with the onion and scallions, and season with the salt and grinds of black pepper. Cook, tossing regularly, until the potato rounds become mildly crunchy and golden, approximately five minutes.
3. Pile the shredded Montasio on top of the vegetables. Slide a metal spatula under some of the potatoes and turn them over, incorporating some of the cheese. Turn all the slices over and over this way, until the cheese shreds are well distributed. With the spatula, clean the sides of the frying pan, and smooth the vegetables and cheese into a neat pancakelike disk, filling the pan bottom.
4. Reduce the heat, and allow the frico to cook, uninterrupted, as the cheese melts and crisps, until the bottom is thoroughly browned and crusted, approximately five minutes. Shake the pan to loosen the disk, put a big plate on top, and invert, dropping the frico onto the plate, then slide it back into the frying pan, top side down. Cook until the second side is crisp and brown, approximately five minutes more.
5. Slide (or invert) the frico onto the plate, and blot up surplus oil from the cheese using a paper towel. Cut into six wedges, and serve instantly.

Lentil Crostini

Crostini con Lenticchie (Italian Name of the Recipe)

Yield: Servings 6

Ingredients:

- ¼ teaspoon crushed red pepper flakes, or to taste
- 1 cup chopped onion
- 1 cup small lentils, preferably lenticchie di Castelluccio
- 12 slices Italian bread
- 2 cups canned Italian plum tomatoes, preferably San Marzano, crushed by hand
- 2 fresh bay leaves
- 2 medium celery stalks, with leaves, finely chopped (approximately 1 cup)
- 2 plump garlic cloves, sliced
- 2 teaspoons kosher salt
- 6 tablespoons extra-virgin olive oil, plus more for drizzling

Directions:

1. Wash the lentils, and put them in a big deep cooking pan with the celery, bay leaves, and 3 cups cold water. Bring to its boiling point, cover the pan, and adjust the heat to maintain a gentle, steady simmer. Cook until the lentils are almost tender, approximately twenty minutes (or longer, depending on size).

2. In the meantime, pour 4 tablespoons of the olive oil into a medium frying pan, and set it on moderate heat. Mix in the garlic and onion, and cook for five minutes or more, until the onion is tender and glistening. Drop the red pepper flakes into a hot spot in the pan, and let it toast for one minute; then mix in the crushed tomatoes, season with a teaspoon of the salt, and bring the sauce to a simmer. Let it bubble gently about five minutes, until a little thickened.
3. When the lentils are just a little undercooked, pour the tomato sauce into the deep cooking pan and stir into the lentils. Return the sauce to a simmer, and cook, partially covered, until the lentils are fully cooked and tender, approximately ten minutes. Take the cover, fish out bay leaves, mix in the rest of the teaspoon salt, and let the lentils cook slowly, stirring regularly, until they're very thick and beginning to fall apart, another ten minutes or so. Take the pan from the heat, and mix in the rest of the 2 tablespoons olive oil.
4. For crostini, grill or toast the bread slices, spoon a mound of lentils on each crostino, and sprinkle on slightly of fine olive oil.

Lettuce and Bread Quiches

Tortini Salati di Lattuga e Pane (Italian Name of the Recipe)

Makes 10

Ingredients:

- ¼ cup bread crumbs
- ½ cup freshly grated Grana Padano
- ½ cup milk
- ¾ teaspoon kosher salt
- 1 bunch scallions, trimmed and chopped (approximately 1 cup)
- 1 tablespoon fresh thyme leaves, chopped
- 1½ cups ½-inch bread cubes
- 3 tablespoons extra-virgin olive oil
- 5 big eggs
- Outer leaves from 1 head romaine lettuce, coarsely chopped (about 3 cups) (save the heart for salad)
- Pinch of freshly grated nutmeg
- Unsalted butter, softened, for lining the muffin tins

Directions:

1. Preheat your oven to 350 degrees. Brush ten cups of a standard muffin tin with softened butter. Drizzle with the bread crumbs to coat all around, and tap out the surplus.
2. To a big frying pan on moderate to high heat, put in the olive oil. When the oil is hot, put in the scallions and thyme. Season with ½ teaspoon salt. Cook and stir until scallions are wilted, approximately 4 minutes. Put in the lettuce, cover, and cook until wilted, approximately 3

minutes. Uncover, increase heat to high, and cook away any surplus liquid in the pan, approximately one minute. Remove from heat when the lettuce still has a little bite to it. Scrape into a container, and let cool.
3. In a large container, whisk together the eggs, milk, nutmeg, ¼ cup grated cheese, and rest of the ¼ teaspoon salt. Mix in the bread cubes and the cooled lettuce mixture, and let soak five minutes.
4. Spoon solids into the lined muffin cups to distribute uniformly, then pour in the egg mixture. Drizzle the tops with the grated cheese. Bake until golden on top and set throughout, approximately twenty minutes. Cool on a rack for five to ten minutes, then loosen the sides using a paring knife before you serve. These are good warm or at room temperature.
5. Use the crusts from the bread you use for cubes to make the bread crumbs to line the muffin tin. If they are too tender, dry them out in a 350-degree oven for five to ten minutes.

Mussels In Spicy Tomato Sauce

Cozze al Pomodoro Piccante (Italian Name of the Recipe)

Yield: Servings 4 To 6

Ingredients:

- ½ teaspoon dried oregano, preferably Sicilian on the branch
- ½ teaspoon kosher salt
- ½ teaspoon peperoncino flakes
- 10 big fresh basil leaves, shredded
- 3 pounds mussels, scrubbed, debearded, and drained
- 6 tablespoons extra-virgin olive oil
- 8 garlic cloves, sliced
- One 28-ounce can Italian plum tomatoes, preferably San Marzano, crushed by hand or a food mill

Directions:

1. Heat 5 tablespoons olive oil in a big Dutch oven on moderate to high heat. Put in the sliced garlic, and cook until the garlic sizzles and turns just golden around the edges, approximately 2 minutes. Put in the tomatoes, slosh out the can with ¼ cup water, and put in that to the pot. Season with the oregano, salt, and peperoncino. Bring to its boiling point, and simmer until a little thickened, approximately ten minutes.
2. Once the sauce has thickened, put in the mussels, stir, and adjust the heat so the sauce is simmering. Cover, and simmer until the mussels open, approximately five minutes.
3. Once the mussels have opened (discard any that have not), mix in the basil, and sprinkle with the rest of the

tablespoon of olive oil. Move the mussels to a serving container, and pour juices over them. Serve instantly.

Prosciutto and Fig Bruschetta

Bruschetta di Prosciutto e Fichi (Italian Name of the Recipe)

Yield: Servings 6

Ingredients:

- 6 long, thin slices Prosciutto di San Daniele or Prosciutto di Parma, or as needed
- 6 slices grilled country bread
- Aceto Balsamico Tradizionale, for drizzling (not necessary)
- Freshly ground black pepper
- ten to 12 ripe fresh green or black figs

Directions:

1. Wipe the figs clean using a damp cloth or paper towel. Cut the figs crosswise into ⅛-inch-thick rounds.
2. Cover the grilled bread with overlapping fig slices. Drape the prosciutto to cover the figs. Grind some black pepper over the prosciutto, sprinkle with the balsamic if you wish, and serve instantly.

Provolone Turnovers

Seadas (Italian Name of the Recipe)
Makes 12

Ingredients:

- ½ teaspoon kosher salt
- 2 tablespoons extra-virgin olive oil
- 3 cups durum-wheat flour
- 3 tablespoons unsalted butter, at room temperature, cut into little chunks
- 9 ounces provolone, in 12 slices
- Honey, for drizzling (not necessary)
- Vegetable oil, for frying

Directions:

1. Put the flour, salt, olive oil, and butter chunks in a food-processor bowl. Process until the fat has been blended and the mixture has a sandy texture. While the processor runs, pour 1 cup minus 2 tablespoons water through the feed tube, and process just until a dough forms and gathers on the blade and cleans the sides of the container. If the dough is too sticky, put in another tablespoon or two of flour; if too dry, put in 2 tablespoons water. Process for a short duration, until the dough comes together; turn it out on a mildly floured surface, and knead by hand a few times, until it's smooth

and tender. Push dough into a disk, wrap well using plastic wrap, and allow to rest at room temperature for minimum half an hour.
2. To make the seadas: Chop the rested dough in half. On a mildly floured surface, roll each piece out to a rectangular sheet approximately 12 by 16 inches; the dough must be about ¼ inch thick. Push a 3-inch round cookie cutter lightly on one sheet of dough but do not cut through it, making twelve marks. Break each provolone slice into three or four pieces, and place them, overlapping, to fit inside one of the traced circles, leaving space around the edges.
3. Roll the other half of the dough to around the same size as the first. Pick it up and drape it over the bottom dough, covering all the rounds of sliced cheese. Lightly press the top sheet around the cheese layers so the edges are distinct. Immerse the cookie cutter in flour, center it over one portion of cheese, and cut through both layers of dough, to the work surface, cutting out one seada. Cut all of them similarly, then pull away the surplus dough between them. Pinch the edges of each seada, securing the cheese inside.
4. Pour vegetable oil into the big frying pan to a depth of ½ inch, and set it on moderate heat. Allow the oil to heat progressively until a piece of dough begins to sizzle when dipped in but does not darken instantly. Cautiously slide as many of the seadas into the pan as fit comfortably, with some space between them. Fry until crisp and

golden, approximately two to three minutes per side. If the cheese starts to leak out during frying, flip the seadas to the other side. Drain the seadas on paper towels, and keep them warm in a low oven. Serve instantly, sprinkled with honey if you prefer.

Rice and Zucchini Crostata

Crostata di Riso e Zucchine (Italian Name of the Recipe)

Makes 15 Or More Appetizer Slices Or Several Dozen Hors D'oeuvres

Ingredients:

FOR THE DOUGH

- ⅓ cup cold water, plus more as needed
- ½ cup extra-virgin olive oil
- 1 teaspoon kosher salt
- 2 cups all-purpose flour, plus more for rolling out the dough

FOR THE FILLING

- ½ cup Italian short-grain rice, such as Arborio, Carnaroli, or Vialone Nano
- 1 cup freshly grated Grana Padano
- 1 pound small zucchini

- 2 bunches scallions, trimmed and finely chopped (about 2 cups)
- 2 cups milk
- 2 cups ricotta, preferably fresh, drained overnight
- 2 teaspoons kosher salt
- 3 big eggs, lightly beaten
- Unsalted butter, for the baking pan

Directions:

1. To make the dough: Pour the flour and salt into a food processor fitted with the metal blade. Pulse a few seconds to aerate the dough. Combine the oil and water together and, with the processor running, pour the liquid through the feed tube and mix for approximately half a minute, until a tender dough forms and gathers on the blade. If it doesn't form, the dough is probably too dry, so put in more water in small amounts until you have a smooth, very tender dough.
2. Turn the dough out onto a mildly floured surface, and knead by hand for one minute. Pat into a rectangle, and wrap loosely using plastic wrap. Allow to rest at room temperature for half an hour.
3. To make the filling: Shred the zucchini on the coarse holes of a box grater into a large container. Toss the rice and shredded zucchini together, and let sit for half an hour to an hour, until the grains have absorbed the vegetable liquid. Fold in the ricotta (breaking up any

lumps), then the grated cheese, scallions, beaten eggs, milk, and salt, stirring thoroughly until combined.
4. Preheat your oven to 375 degrees. Spread the butter on the bottom and sides of a 12-by-18-inch rimmed sheet pan.
5. On a mildly floured surface, roll the dough to a rectangle minimum 4 inches longer and wider than the baking sheet. Move the dough to the pan, either by folding it in quarters and lifting it onto the sheet, or by rolling it up around the floured rolling pin and then unfolding it on the baking sheet. When the dough is centered over the pan, softly push its center flat against the bottom, and rim the pan, leaving even flaps of overhanging dough on all sides.
6. Scrape the filling into the dough-lined pan, and spread it to fill the crust in a uniform layer. Fold the dough flaps over the top of the filling, pleating the corners, to make a top-crust border that resembles a picture frame, with the filling uncovered in the middle.
7. Place the pan in your oven, and bake until the crust is deep golden brown and the filling is set, forty-five minutes to an hour. About midway through the baking time, turn the pan in the oven, back to front, for uniform color and cooking. Cool the crostata on a wire rack for minimum half an hour to set the filling before slicing. The crostata can be served warm or at room temperature, cut into pieces in any shape you prefer.

Rice Balls

Arancini di Riso (Italian Name of the Recipe)
Makes About 24

Ingredients:

- ½ teaspoon kosher salt, plus more for seasoning
- 1 cup all-purpose flour
- 1 cup dry white wine
- 1 cup finely diced ham or prosciutto (about 3 ounces)
- 1 cup freshly grated Grana Padano
- 1 cup frozen peas, thawed
- 1 medium onion, chopped
- 10 basil leaves, chopped
- 2 big eggs
- 2 cups Arborio rice
- 2 cups fine dried bread crumbs
- 3 tablespoons extra-virgin olive oil
- 4 ounces fresh mozzarella, cut into 24 cubes
- 5 cups Chicken Stock
- Vegetable oil, for frying

Directions:

1. In a small pot, warm chicken stock over low heat. In a moderate-sized deep cooking pan, heat the olive oil. When the oil is hot, put in the onion and cook until it starts to soften, approximately three to four minutes. Put

in the ham or prosciutto, and cook a few minutes, until it starts to render its fat. Put in the rice, and cook to coat it in the oil and fat. Pour in the wine, bring to a simmer, and cook until the wine is almost reduced away. Put in 3 cups of the hot chicken stock and the salt. Cover, and simmer until the chicken stock is absorbed by the rice, approximately seven to eight minutes. Put in the rest of the 2 cups stock, and cover once more. Cook until rice is al dente, approximately six to seven minutes more. Uncover; if any liquid remains, increase heat and cook until all of the liquid is absorbed, one more minute or two. Mix in peas, and spread rice on a rimmed sheet pan to cool.
2. Once the rice cools down, put in a container and stir in grated cheese and chopped basil. Scoop out about ⅓ cup rice, and place a cube of mozzarella in the center, making a firm ball around the cheese. You should get about twenty-four arancini.
3. Spread the flour and bread crumbs on two rimmed plates. Beat the eggs in a shallow container. Dredge the arancini in the flour, tapping off the surplus. Immerse them in the beaten egg, allowing the surplus drip back into the container. Roll in bread crumbs to coat completely.
4. In a big straight-sided frying pan, heat 1 inch vegetable oil on moderate heat until the tip of an arancino sizzles on contact. Fry arancini in batches, taking care not to crowd the frying pan, turning on all sides, until golden,

approximately 3 minutes per batch. Drain over paper towels, and sprinkle with salt while still warm.

Ricotta Frittata

Frittata con Ricotta (Italian Name of the Recipe)

Yield: Servings 4 To 6

Ingredients:

- ½ cup freshly grated Grana Padano
- ½ teaspoon kosher salt
- 1 big onion, sliced ¼ inch thick
- 1 big ripe tomato, sliced ½ inch thick
- 3 tablespoons extra-virgin olive oil
- 6 tablespoons fresh ricotta
- 8 big basil leaves, shredded
- 8 big eggs

Directions:

1. Preheat your oven to 375 degrees. Heat the oil in a 10-inch nonstick frying pan on moderate heat. Put in onion and cook until softened, approximately five to six minutes. Push onion slices to one side of the frying pan, and lay the tomato slices in one layer in the cleared space. Sear the tomato, flipping over once, until the slices soften just at the edges, approximately half a

minute per side. Transfer the tomatoes to a plate, and let onions carry on cooking while preparing the eggs.
2. In a container, beat the eggs with the salt. Mix in the basil and ¼ cup of the grated cheese until thoroughly combined. Spread the onion slices in a uniform layer in the bottom of the frying pan, and pour the eggs on top. Decrease the heat to moderate low, and allow to cook until the eggs start to set around the edges of the pan, approximately two to three minutes. Position tomato slices on top of the frittata, and drop tablespoons of the ricotta between the tomato slices. Drizzle all over with the rest of the grated cheese. Bake frittata until it is set all the way through and the top is golden, approximately eighteen minutes.
3. Allow to rest for a few minutes; then run a knife around the edge of the frying pan, and slide frittata onto a plate or cutting board. Serve in wedges, warm or at room temperature.

Roasted Pepper Rolls Stuffed With Tuna

Peperoni Farciti con Tonno ed Acciughe (Italian Name of the Recipe)

Makes About 15 Small Rolls, Serving 6 As An Hors D'oeuvre

Ingredients:

- ⅓ cup extra-virgin olive oil, plus more as needed

- ⅓ cup mayonnaise
- 1 tablespoon apple-cider vinegar
- 1 tablespoon chopped fresh Italian parsley
- 1 tablespoon Dijon mustard
- 1 teaspoon kosher salt
- 2 small anchovy fillets, drained and finely chopped
- 2 tablespoons small drained capers, finely chopped
- 3 or 4 sweet red or assorted-color peppers (approximately 1½ pounds total)
- Two 6-ounce cans tuna in olive oil (preferably imported from Italy)

Directions:

1. Preheat your oven to 350 degreees. Rub the peppers all over with 2 tablespoons olive oil, season with ½ teaspoon salt, and place on a parchment-lined baking sheet. Roast for half an hour or soflipping over the peppers once in a while, until their skins are wrinkled and mildly charred.
2. Allow the peppers to cool to room temperature. Cut in half (through the stem end), discard the stem and seeds, peel off the skin, and slice the halves along the length into strips 2 inches wide. Scrape any rest of the seeds from the strips, swiftly wash the strips under cold water, and place them in a sieve to drain and dry.
3. To make the stuffing: Drain the tuna, and break it into flakes in a moderate-sized container. Combine the chopped anchovies, capers, vinegar, mustard,

mayonnaise, parsley, 2 tablespoons olive oil, and about ½ teaspoon salt into the tuna using a fork. Stir rapidly, breaking up lumps of fish, until the stuffing is tender and quite smooth.
4. Drop a small tablespoon of stuffing at one end of each roasted pepper strip, and roll it up tightly, making a neat cylinder. Push the pepper as you wrap, so it sticks to itself and stays closed.
5. To serve: arrange all the rolls on a platter, sprinkle a little extra olive oil all over, and drizzle lightly with coarse salt.

Rosemary and Lemon Focaccia

Focaccia al Rosmarino e Limone (Italian Name of the Recipe)

Yield: Servings 8

Ingredients:

- ½ lemon, cut into quarters and thinly sliced
- 1 package active dry yeast (2¼ teaspoons)
- 2¼ teaspoons kosher salt
- 5 cups all-purpose flour, plus more as needed
- 5 tablespoons extra-virgin olive oil, plus more for brushing
- Leaves of 2 sprigs fresh rosemary, half chopped, half left whole
- Pinch of sugar

- Zest of 1 lemon

Directions:

1. Dissolve yeast and sugar in ½ cup warm water (approximately 100 degrees) until a little bubbly, approximately five minutes. Once the yeast is bubbly, put in 3 tablespoons olive oil and 1½ cups room-temperature water.
2. In the container of a mixer fitted using the paddle attachment, put the 5 cups flour and 2 teaspoons salt. Pour in the yeast mixture, and put in the lemon zest and chopped rosemary. Mix at low speed until blended. Switch to the dough hook, and knead at moderate speed until the dough gathers on the hook and is smooth and springy, approximately 6 minutes, adding a little more flour or water if necessary. Move the dough to an oiled container, cover, and let rise at room temperature until doubled, approximately 1½ hours.
3. Punch the dough down. Brush a rimmed half-sheet pan with olive oil, and press the dough into the pan all the way to the edges. Cover loosely using plastic wrap, and let rise until doubled, approximately forty-five minutes.
4. Preheat your oven to 450 degrees. In a small container, toss the lemon pieces, reserved whole rosemary leaves, rest of the ¼ teaspoon salt, and rest of the 2 tablespoons olive oil together. Push dimples all over the focaccia with your finger. Scatter the oil-rosemary mixture uniformly over the risen dough. Bake on the bottom rack of the

oven until the focaccia is thoroughly cooked and golden brown on the bottom, approximately twenty to twenty-five minutes. Take out of the pan, and cool on a rack.

VARIATION: FOCACCIA FILLED WITH SOPPRESSATA AND PROVOLONE

Focaccia Farcita con Soppressata e Provola (Italian Name of the Recipe)

Yield: Servings 8

Ingredients:

- 1 recipe focaccia dough from preceding recipe, made without lemon and rosemary
- 2 tablespoons extra-virgin olive oil
- 4 big hard-boiled eggs, sliced
- 4 ounces sliced provolone
- 4 ounces soppressata, thinly sliced

Directions:

1. After the first rise (see preceding recipe), brush a 9-by-13-inch baking dish with 1 tablespoon olive oil. Punch the dough down, and split it in half. Push half of the dough into the oiled dish, all the way to the edges, with an edge of about ½ inch pressed up the sides. Layer the soppressata, almost to the edges. Layer the cheese similarly over the soppressata, and layer the sliced egg over the cheese.

2. Roll or press the rest of the dough to approximately 9 by 13 inches, and layer on top of the provolone. Push all around the edges to secure. Poke holes in the dough in five or six places using a paring knife. Softly brush focaccia with rest of the olive oil.
3. Cover using plastic wrap, and let rise half an hour. Preheat your oven to 375 degrees. After the second rise, remove plastic, cover the dish with foil, and bake until dough is puffed but not yet colored, approximately twenty minutes.
4. Uncover, and bake until dough is thoroughly cooked and golden from head to toe, approximately twenty to twenty-five minutes. Allow to cool in the baking dish on a rack minimum fifteen minutes before cutting into squares and serving, either warm or at room temperature.

VARIATION: FOCACCIA FILLED WITH SPECK AND FONTINA

Focaccia con Speck e Fontina (Italian Name of the Recipe)

Yield: Servings 8

Ingredients:

- 1 recipe focaccia dough, made without lemon and rosemary
- 2 tablespoons extra-virgin olive oil
- 4 big hard-boiled eggs, sliced (not necessary)

- 4 ounces Italian Fontina, sliced
- 4 ounces speck, sliced

Directions:

1. After the first rise, brush a 9-by-13-inch baking dish with 1 tablespoon olive oil. Punch the dough down, and split it in half. Push half of the dough down into the oiled dish, all the way to the edges, with an edge of about ½ inch pressed up the sides. Layer the speck, almost to the edges. Layer the egg slices, if using, on top. Layer the cheese similarly over the speck.
2. Roll or press the rest of the dough to approximately 9 by 13 inches, and layer on top of the Fontina. Push all around the edges to secure. Poke holes in the dough in five or six places using a paring knife. Softly brush the focaccia with rest of the olive oil.
3. Cover using plastic wrap, and let rise half an hour. Preheat your oven to 375 degrees. After the second rise, remove plastic, cover the dish with foil, and bake until dough is puffed but not yet colored, approximately twenty minutes.
4. Uncover, and bake until dough is thoroughly cooked and golden from head to toe, approximately twenty to twenty-five minutes. Allow to cool in the baking dish on a rack minimum fifteen minutes before cutting into squares and serving, either warm or at room temperature.

Sausage Crostini

Crostini con Salsicce (Italian Name of the Recipe)
Makes 8, Serving 4

Ingredients:

- ¼ cup freshly shredded Grana Padano
- ¼ teaspoon ground fennel seeds
- ½ cup dry white wine
- 1 cup diced celery
- 2 tablespoons extra-virgin olive oil
- 3 sweet Italian sausages, removed from casings (approximately 12 ounces)
- 4 ounces shredded Taleggio or Fontina, plus 2 ounces thinly sliced
- Four ½-inch-thick slices day-old country bread, approximately 4 by 6 inches, halved

Directions:

1. Preheat your oven to 400 degrees. To a big frying pan on moderate heat, put in the olive oil. When the oil is hot, put in the sausage and celery, and cook until browned, approximately 4 minutes.
2. Put in the white wine, and adjust the heat so it simmers rapidly. Cook until wine has reduced away, approximately 2 minutes. Scrape into a moderate-sized container and let cool to room temperature.

3. When it is cooled, put in the shredded Taleggio, the grated Grana Padano, and the ground fennel, and toss thoroughly. Position the sliced bread on a baking sheet, and top with the sausage mixture. Top that with the sliced Taleggio. Bake until edges of the bread are toasted and the cheese is browned, approximately seven minutes. Serve hot.

Sausage, Bread, and Pepper Frittata

Frittata con Salsiccia e Peperoni (Italian Name of the Recipe)

Yield: Servings 4 To 6

Ingredients:

- ¼ cup freshly grated Grana Padano
- ¼ cup milk
- ½ teaspoon kosher salt
- 1 big bunch scallions, trimmed and cut into ½-inch pieces
- 1 red bell pepper, cut in ½-inch strips
- 1½ cups ½-inch cubes from day-old loaf of country bread
- 3 tablespoons extra-virgin olive oil
- 8 big eggs
- 8 ounces sweet Italian sausage, removed from casings (about 2 links)

Directions:

1. Preheat your oven to 375 degrees. Heat a medium (10-inch) nonstick frying pan on moderate heat. Put in the olive oil. When the oil is hot, cook the sausage, crumbling with the back of a wooden spoon until no longer pink, approximately three to four minutes. Put in the scallions, season with ¼ teaspoon salt, and cook, stirring, until the scallions start to wilt, approximately two to three minutes. Put in bell pepper and cook, stirring, until wilted but not completely limp, approximately eight to ten minutes.
2. In the meantime, in a container, beat eggs with the milk and rest of the salt. Let the bread cubes soak in the egg-milk mixture until moistened, approximately two to three minutes. Decrease the heat under frying pan to moderate low, then pour in the egg mixture and the bread, and allow to cook until the eggs start to set around the edges of the pan, approximately two to three minutes.
3. Drizzle all over with the grated cheese. Put the frying pan in the oven, and bake until the frittata is set all the way through and the top is golden, approximately eighteen minutes. Allow to rest for a few minutes, then run a knife around the edge of the frying pan and invert frittata onto a plate or cutting board. Serve in wedges, warm or at room temperature.

Scrambled Eggs and Asparagus

Frittata di Asparagi e Uova (Italian Name of the Recipe)

Yield: Servings 4

Ingredients:

- 1 pound pencil-thin asparagus
- 2 tablespoons extra-virgin olive oil
- 8 big eggs
- Kosher salt and freshly ground black pepper

Directions:

1. Remove and discard the tough lower ends of the asparagus. Chop the spears into 2-inch lengths. In a big nonstick frying pan, sauté the asparagus spears in olive oil, sprinkling them lightly with salt. Cover the pan and cook on moderate heat, stirring once in a while, until asparagus is tender but still firm, approximately five minutes.
2. Beat the eggs lightly in a container with salt and pepper. Put in the eggs to the asparagus, scrambling the mixture lightly using a fork. Cook two minutes or less, depending on the texture desired, and serve instantly.

Steamed Mussels In Savory Wine Sauce

Cozze al Vino Bianco (Italian Name of the Recipe)

Yield: Servings 6

Ingredients:

- ¼ to ½ cup dried bread crumbs, or as needed
- ½ cup dry white wine
- ½ teaspoon kosher salt
- ½ teaspoon peperoncino, or to taste
- 1 big onion, sliced ½ inch thick
- 3 pounds mussels, scrubbed, debearded, and drained
- 3 tablespoons chopped fresh Italian parsley
- 4 fresh bay leaves
- 4 garlic cloves, crushed and peeled
- 6 tablespoons extra-virgin olive oil

Directions:

1. Pour 4 tablespoons olive oil into a big deep cooking pan, drop in the crushed garlic, and set on moderate heat. When the garlic is fragrant and sizzling, mix in the onion slices, bay leaves, salt, and peperoncino. Cook for about 2 minutes, tossing and stirring, just until the onion starts to wither but still has some crunch. Pour in the wine, and bring to its boiling point. Instantly dump all the mussels into the pan, tumble them over swiftly, cover firmly, and Increase the heat. Steam the mussels for about three minutes, regularly shaking the covered pan, then toss them over, with a wire spider or wide slotted spoon. If the mussel shells have already opened (or almost all are

open), leave the pan uncovered—otherwise, replace the cover and steam slightly longer.
2. Once the mussels have steamed open, drizzle ¼ cup bread crumbs all over the pan. Swiftly tumble the mussels over and over, still using high heat, so their liquor and the crumbs fall into the bubbling pan juices and create a sauce. (If the pan sauce is still thin after one minute of bubbling, drizzle in more bread crumbs.) Remove bay leaves and garlic cloves.
3. To finish, sprinkle rest of the 2 tablespoons olive oil and drizzle the chopped parsley on top, and toss briefly to distribute the seasonings. Turn off the heat, set the pan in the center of the table, and allow the people to scoop mussels and sauce into their own warm soup bowls.

Stuffed Artichokes

Carciofi Ripieni (Italian Name of the Recipe)

Yield: Servings 6

Ingredients:

- ⅛ teaspoon crushed red pepper flakes
- ½ cup freshly grated Grana Padano
- ½ cup pine nuts, toasted and coarsely chopped
- ½ cup plus 2 tablespoons chopped fresh Italian parsley
- ½ cup plus 3 tablespoons extra-virgin olive oil
- ¾ teaspoon kosher salt

- 1 cup dry white wine
- 1½ cups fine dried bread crumbs
- 2 big hard-boiled eggs, finely chopped
- 6 big artichokes
- Grated zest from 1 lemon (save lemon for juicing)
- Juice of 2 lemons, freshly squeezed

Directions:

1. Preheat your oven to 400 degrees. To clean and prepare the artichokes, fill a container with approximately a quart of cold water, and put in the juice of one lemon, plus the squeezed-out lemon halves. Peel and trim the stem of the first artichoke, save the stem, and put artichoke and stem in the lemon water. Pull off any tough outer leaves and discard. Use a paring knife to trim away any tough parts around the base and stem of the artichoke. Use a serrated knife to cut off the top third of the artichoke and discard. Push the leaves out to expose the fuzzy purple choke. Use a small spoon to scrape out the choke to expose the heart. Put the prepared artichoke in the container of water and lemon juice to keep it from oxidizing. Repeat with rest of the artichokes.
2. For the stuffing: In a moderate-sized container, combine the bread crumbs, grated cheese, and chopped pine nuts. Mix in ½ cup of the parsley, ½ cup of the olive oil, the eggs, ¼ teaspoon salt, and the reserved lemon zest. Toss using a fork until the crumbs are moistened with the olive oil.

3. Take the cleaned artichokes from the water, and drain them upside down on a kitchen towel. Spread the leaves of an artichoke open, by lightly prying using your fingers, and fill the center with the stuffing. Carry on working outward, sprinkling and packing stuffing into the rows of leaves as you separate them. Once stuffed, set the artichoke in a baking dish that will hold all six tightly. Repeat with the rest of the artichokes.
4. Pour the wine and 1 cup water around the artichokes, and put in the rest of the lemon juice and artichoke stems. Season the liquid with the rest of the salt and the crushed red pepper flakes. Sprinkle the rest of the 3 tablespoons of olive oil over the artichokes. Tent the dish with foil, and bake for about half an hour. Uncover, and bake until the artichokes are tender all the way through and the crumbs are browned and crusty, approximately twenty minutes to half an hour more. If the cooking juices are too thin, set the baking pan with artichokes on the stove and boil for a few minutes to reduce the sauce to your preference. Mix in the rest of the 2 tablespoons of chopped parsley. Serve the artichokes in shallow soup plates, surrounded with the cooking juices.

Stuffed Mushrooms

Funghi Ripieni (Italian Name of the Recipe)

Yield: Servings 6

Ingredients:

- ¼ cup dry white wine
- ¼ cup finely chopped fresh Italian parsley
- ½ cup Chicken Stock or Vegetable Stock
- ½ cup coarse bread crumbs
- ½ cup finely chopped red bell pepper
- ½ cup finely chopped scallions
- ½ cup freshly grated Grana Padano
- 2 tablespoons extra-virgin olive oil, plus more for drizzling
- 24 white or cremini mushrooms, each approximately 1½ inches in diameter
- 4 tablespoons unsalted butter
- Kosher salt and freshly ground black pepper

Directions:

1. Preheat your oven to 425 degrees. Take the stems from the mushrooms, and finely cut the stems. Heat 2 tablespoons of the olive oil in a moderate-sized pan on moderate heat. Put in the scallions, and cook until wilted, approximately one minute. Mix in the red pepper and chopped mushroom stems, and cook, stirring, until soft, approximately 3 minutes. Remove to a container and let cool.
2. Toss the bread crumbs, grated cheese, 2 tablespoons of the parsley, and the cooled sautéed vegetables until completely mixed. Sprinkle salt and pepper to taste. Stuff

the cavity of each mushroom with the filling, pushing it in with a teaspoon until even with the sides of the mushroom.
3. Using 2 tablespoons of the butter, grease a baking pan. Position the mushrooms side by side in the pan and, using the rest of the 2 tablespoons butter, dot the top of each mushroom with approximately ¼ teaspoon butter. Put in the stock, wine, and rest of the parsley to the pan. Sprinkle the tops of the mushrooms with olive oil. Bake until the mushrooms are thoroughly cooked and the bread crumbs are golden brown, approximately twenty minutes. Serve the mushrooms on a warmed platter, or split them among warmed plates. Pour the pan juices into a small deep cooking pan, and bring to its boiling point on top of the stove. Reduce until it becomes slightly thick, to the consistency of gravy, one to two minutes. Spoon the juices over the mushrooms, before you serve.

Stuffed Olives Ascolane

Olive Ascolane Ripiene (Italian Name of the Recipe)

Yield: Servings 6

Ingredients:

STUFFING

- ¼ cup fine dried bread crumbs
- ¼ cup freshly grated Grana Padano
- ½ cup dry white wine
- 1 big egg, beaten
- 1 tablespoon extra-virgin olive oil
- 8 ounces sweet Italian sausage without fennel seeds

OLIVES

- 1 cup all-purpose flour
- 2 big eggs
- 2 cups fine dried bread crumbs
- 3 cups big green pitted olives, such as Ascolane
- Kosher salt
- Vegetable oil, for frying

Directions:

1. For the stuffing: In a moderate-sized frying pan, heat the olive oil on moderate to high heat. Put in the sausage. Cook and crumble using a wooden spoon until thoroughly cooked, approximately five minutes. Increase heat to high, put in the white wine, and cook until absorbed, approximately 3 minutes. Scrape into a moderate-sized container, and crumble sausage using a fork until very fine and crumbly. Let cool to room temperature.
2. To the sausage, put in one egg, the grated cheese, and bread crumbs. Mix thoroughly.

3. For the olives: In a deep pot, heat 2 inches of vegetable oil to 365 degrees. Line a sheet pan with parchment.
4. Push the stuffing into the cavities in the olives, filling to the brim and packing the stuffing firmly. Put the flour, two eggs, and bread crumbs into three different shallow containers. Dredge the olives in flour, and then in the whisked eggs, allowing the surplus drip back into the container. Roll to coat them in the bread crumbs, and rest on the sheet pan while you bread the rest of the olives.
5. When all of the olives are breaded, fry, in three batches, until the breading is crisp and golden, approximately three to four minutes per batch. Drain over paper towels, and sprinkle lightly with salt if required.

Stuffed Zucchini Blossoms

Fiori di Zucchine Ripieni (Italian Name of the Recipe)

Yield: Servings 6

Ingredients:

BLOSSOMS

- ¼ cup freshly grated Grana Padano
- 1 cup fresh ricotta
- 24 zucchini blossoms
- Grated zest of 1 small lemon

- Kosher salt and freshly ground black pepper

BATTER

- 1 teaspoon baking powder
- 1 teaspoon kosher salt
- 1½ cups all-purpose flour
- One 12-ounce bottle amber beer, or 1½ cups seltzer
- Vegetable oil, for frying

Directions:

1. Lightly pry open the zucchini blossoms, pull out the small yellow stamen from inside each, and discard. In a small container, mix together the ricotta, grated cheese, and lemon zest, and sprinkle with salt and pepper.
2. To stuff the blossoms, open the flowers and stuff with approximately 2 teaspoons or so of the ricotta mixture. Fold over the ends to close and secure the filling in the blossoms.
3. For the batter: In a moderate-sized container, whisk together the flour, baking powder, and salt. Whisk in the beer to make a smooth batter; allow to rest five minutes.
4. In the meantime, in a deep pot, heat 2 inches of vegetable oil to 360 degrees. Once the batter has rested, dip the blossoms in the batter one by one, allowing the surplus drip back into the container. Fry in two or three batches, depending on the size of your pot, until the batter is crisp and golden, approximately three to four

minutes per batch, flipping over to brown both sides. Drain over paper towels, sprinkle with salt while hot, and repeat with the rest of the blossoms and batter.
5. Serve alone or atop a thin layer of hot marinara sauce.

Swiss Chard and Potato Crostata

Crostata con Bietole e Patate (Italian Name of the Recipe)

Yield: Servings 8 To 12

Ingredients:

DOUGH

- ⅓ cup cold water, plus more as needed
- ½ cup extra-virgin olive oil
- ½ teaspoon kosher salt
- 2 cups all-purpose flour, plus more for rolling the dough

FILLING

- 1 bunch Swiss chard, including stems, approximately 1½ pounds, washed and drained
- 1 cup freshly grated Grana Padano
- 1 cup heavy cream
- 2 cups grated low-moisture mozzarella
- 2 potatoes, approximately 1½ pounds total

- 2 teaspoons kosher salt
- 3 tablespoons extra-virgin olive oil
- 4 big eggs

Directions:

1. For the dough: Use a food processor to mix the flour and salt, and pulse. Combine the oil and water together, and with the machine running, put in oil and water mixture, and process to make a smooth, tender dough, approximately half a minute. Put in more flour or water if necessary, until the dough pulls off the sides of the food processor and forms a ball around the blade. The dough must be tender and a little sticky to the touch.
2. Dump the dough onto a mildly floured work surface, and knead until very smooth, approximately 1 minute, sprinkling barely sufficient flour so you can roll the dough into a smooth ball. Cover the dough with plastic wrap, and allow to rest at room temperature for half an hour. (Dough can also be made a day ahead and refrigerated; let come to room temperature before rolling.)
3. For the filling: Bring a big pot of salted water to its boiling point. Chop the leaves from the stems of the chard and cut into 1-inch strips. Chop the stems into ½-inch pieces and keep separate. When the water boils, put in the stems and boil for about ten minutes, then put in the leaves, and boil until both are tender, approximately fifteen minutes more. Drain, let cool, then squeeze in

your hands until most of the water is out. Chop, and set aside.

4. In the meantime, put the potatoes in a different pot with water to cover, and simmer for about half an hour until soft when pierced using a fork. Drain. When they are sufficiently cool to handle, peel the potatoes, return them to the pot, and mash, adding the cream and olive oil. Put in the chopped Swiss chard and mix thoroughly. Beat the eggs and salt together, and mix into the potato-chard mixture. Fold in the mozzarella and Grana Padano, and set aside.

5. Preheat your oven to 375 degrees. On a floured surface, roll the dough to fit a rimmed half sheet pan with approximately 3 inches extra on all sides, trimming if necessary. Butter the pan. Fit the dough into the sheet pan, with the extra dough hanging off the sides, and spread the filling uniformly over the dough. Fold the overlap of the dough over to make a 2-inch crust around the pan over the filling, leaving the center without crust. Bake until filling is set and crust is golden, approximately 40 to forty-five minutes. Cool on a rack. Serve a little warm or at room temperature.

Swordfish-Stuffed Peppers

Peperoni Farciti con Pesce Spada (Italian Name of the Recipe)

Yield: Servings 6 As An Appetizer Or Light Main Course

Ingredients:

- ¼ cup chopped fresh Italian parsley
- ½ cup dry white wine
- 1 teaspoon chopped fresh thyme
- 1 teaspoon kosher salt
- 1 teaspoon kosher salt
- 1¼ pounds skinless swordfish steaks, coarsely chopped
- 1½ cups frozen peas
- 2 bunches scallions, trimmed and coarsely chopped (about 2 cups)
- 4 garlic cloves, finely chopped
- 6 cups crustless day-old bread cubes
- 6 small red, yellow, or orange bell peppers
- 6 tablespoons extra-virgin olive oil

Directions:

1. Preheat your oven to 400 degrees. Cut each pepper into thirds along the length, along the natural folds. Take the seeds to make 18 pepper "boats." On a rimmed baking sheet, toss the peppers with 2 tablespoons of the olive oil, and season with ½ teaspoon of the salt.
2. Put the bread cubes in a large container, submerge them in water, and allow them to soak while making the stuffing.

3. To a big frying pan on moderate to high heat, put in the rest of the olive oil. When the oil is hot, put in the swordfish, and season with the rest of the ½ teaspoon salt. Stir to coat the swordfish in the oil, then put in the garlic. Once everything is sizzling, mix in the peas and thyme. Put in the wine, and simmer until it has evaporated, approximately five minutes.
4. Put in the scallions, and cook until they are wilted, approximately 3 minutes. Mix in the parsley. Scrape the mixture into a large container. Squeeze all of the water out of the soaked bread, and crumble the bread into the swordfish mixture. Mix thoroughly, and stuff the filling into the pepper boats. Cover with foil, and bake until set, approximately twenty minutes. Uncover, and bake until the top of the filling is golden brown, approximately twenty minutes more. Serve hot or at room temperature.

Tomato Fritters

Frittelle di Pomodori (Italian Name of the Recipe)

Yield: Servings 6

Ingredients:

- ¼ cup fresh whole basil leaves
- ½ teaspoon baking powder
- ½ teaspoon kosher salt, plus more for seasoning
- 1 big egg, lightly beaten

- 1 cup all-purpose flour, plus more for dredging
- 6 medium under-ripened tomatoes
- Vegetable oil, for frying

Directions:

1. Use a deep pot or Dutch oven to heat several inches of oil to 365 degrees. Cut the tomatoes crosswise into ½-inch-thick slices, sprinkle with salt, and drain thoroughly on paper towels, turning once, while making the batter. Cut the basil leaves.
2. In a large container, whisk together the flour, baking powder, and ½ teaspoon salt. Whisk in the egg and ¾ cup water to make a smooth batter. Whisk in the chopped basil barely sufficient to distribute it in the batter.
3. Spread about a cup of flour on a plate. Pat tomatoes dry one more time, then gently dredge them in the flour, on both sides. Immerse in the batter, and fry, in batches, until the batter is puffed and dark golden, approximately 2 minutes per side. Drain on fresh paper towels, and sprinkle lightly with salt. Serve hot.

Whipped Salt Cod Spread

Baccalà Mantecato (Italian Name of the Recipe)

Makes About 4 Cups

Ingredients:

- ½ cup half-and-half or light cream
- ½ cup poaching water from cooking the baccalà
- 1 cup extra-virgin olive oil
- 1 medium russet potato (about ½ pound)
- 1 pound boneless baccalà (salt cod)
- 2 garlic cloves, thoroughly minced
- Freshly ground black pepper to taste

Directions:

1. Two days before you want to prepare the baccalà, place it in a large container and immerse it in cold water by several inches. Allow it to soak in your refrigerator to remove the salt, changing the water completely every eight to ten hours. When it is adequately soaked, drain and pat dry.
2. Chop the baccalà into smaller pieces—6 inches or so—and put them in a deep cooking pan or deep frying pan with minimum an inch of water to cover. Bring to its boiling point, set the cover ajar (rest it on a wooden spoon set on the rim of the pan), and cook at a steady bubbling boil for approximately twenty minutes, until the cod is easy to flake but still has body and shape. Lift the baccalà out of the cooking water, and allow it to drain and cool in a colander. Reserve ½ cup of the cooking water.
3. In the meantime, wash the potato but leave it whole and unpeeled. Place it in a small pot and cover with cold

water. Bring to the boil, and cook steadily until you can effortlessly pierce the potato using a knife blade, twenty-five minutes to half an hour. Allow it to cool, and peel it.
4. Ready your electric mixer, and flake all the fish into its container. Beat using the paddle at low speed to break the fish up more; drop in the minced garlic and the cooked and peeled potato, and beat at moderate speed while you pour in half the olive oil very progressively. Increase the speed to high, then put in the rest of the oil and whip the fish to lighten it. Decrease the speed to moderate and incorporate the half-and-half progressively; then whip at high speed once more. At this point, the whipped cod must be smooth and fluffy, kind of like mashed potatoes but with texture. If it is too thick, thin it using the cooking water, only as much as gets the job done, no more. To finish, season with pepper and stir it in to combine.

Zucchini Fritters

Frittelle di Zucchine (Italian Name of the Recipe)

Yield: Servings 6

Ingredients:

- ½ teaspoon baking powder
- ½ teaspoon kosher salt, plus more for seasoning
- ⅔ cup all-purpose flour

- 2 medium zucchini (8 ounces), washed and trimmed
- 3 big eggs
- 3 tablespoons chopped fresh Italian parsley
- Grated zest of 1 lemon
- Lemon wedges, for serving
- Vegetable oil, for frying

Directions:

1. In a straight-sided frying pan, heat 1 inch of vegetable oil to 360 degrees. Grate the zucchini on the medium holes of a box grater onto a kitchen towel. Firmly wrap the zucchini in the towel, and wring out as much liquid as you can. Beat the eggs in a large container. Mix in the zucchini, breaking up any clumps using a fork. Mix in the parsley and lemon zest.
2. Sift together the flour, baking powder, and salt. Mix into the egg mixture until just blended—don't overmix.
3. Brush a soup spoon with vegetable oil, and with it drop dollops of batter into the oil, patting the fritters gently using the back of a spatula to flatten a little. Fry, flipping over once, until golden on both sides and thoroughly cooked, approximately 2 minutes per side. Fry them in batches. The fritters are cooked when a fork inserted in the center comes out clean. Drain cooked fritters using paper towels, and sprinkle lightly with salt. Serve fritters immediately, with lemon wedges.

Salads

Caesar Salad	134
Celery Root, Apple, Arugula, and Walnut Salad	136
Celery, Artichoke, and Mortadella Salad	137
Condiggion Salad with Tuna	139
Crab and Celery Salad	140
Cucumber, Potato, and Green Bean Salad	141
Farro Salad with Grilled Eggplant and Peppers	142
Lobster Salad with Fresh Tomatoes	144
Octopus and Potato Salad	146
Pickled Carrots	148
Poached Seafood Salad	149
Puntarelle and Anchovy Salad	151
Radicchio Salad with Orange	153
Raw and Cooked Salad	154
Red Cabbage and Bacon Salad	156
Roasted Beet and Beet Greens Salad with Apples and Goat Cheese	157
Roasted Eggplant and Tomato Salad	159
Salad of Dandelion Greens with Almond Vinaigrette and Dried Ricotta	161
Scallion and Asparagus Salad	162
Seafood and Rice Salad	164
Shaved Fennel, Celery, and Red Onion Salad with Salami	167
Shrimp and Mixed Bean Salad	168
Steamed Broccoli and Egg Salad	169
Striped Bass Salad	170
Tomato and Bread Salad	171
Tripe Salad	172
Warm Mushroom Salad	174

CAESAR SALAD

Insalata alla Caesar (Italian Name of the Recipe)

Yield: Servings 6

Ingredients:

- ⅓ cup extra-virgin olive oil
- ½ cup freshly grated Grana Padano
- ½ teaspoon kosher salt
- 1 tablespoon Dijon mustard
- 2 cups country-bread cubes, approximately ½-inch pieces
- 3 garlic cloves
- 3 heads romaine hearts, cut into 1-inch pieces crosswise
- 4 anchovy fillets
- 4 tablespoons red wine vinegar
- Freshly ground black pepper
- Yolks of 2 big hard-boiled eggs

Directions:

1. Preheat your oven to 350 degrees. Scatter bread cubes on a baking sheet, and toast until crunchy throughout, approximately eight to ten minutes. Set aside to cool.
2. In a mini–food processor, mix the vinegar, egg yolks, garlic, anchovies, and mustard. Process until smooth, scraping down the sides of the work bowl as required. While the processor runs, pour the oil through the feed tube to make a smooth dressing. Sprinkle with salt and pepper.
3. Put the romaine and croutons in a big serving bowl. Sprinkle with the dressing and toss thoroughly. Drizzle with the grated cheese and toss once more. Serve instantly.

CELERY ROOT, APPLE, ARUGULA, AND WALNUT SALAD

Insalata di Sedano Rapa, Mele, Rucola e Noci (Italian Name of the Recipe)

Yield: 4 to 6 Servings

Ingredients:

- ¼ cup extra-virgin olive oil
- ½ cup walnuts, toasted and coarsely chopped
- ½ teaspoon kosher salt
- 1 big Granny Smith apple, julienned (skin on)

- 1 medium celery root, peeled and julienned
- 4 anchovy fillets, finely chopped
- Freshly ground black pepper
- Juice of 1 big lemon, freshly squeezed
- One 5-ounce package baby arugula

Directions:

1. In a big bowl, whisk together the anchovies and lemon juice to dissolve the anchovies. Whisk in the salt, and flavor with pepper. Whisk in the olive oil to make a smooth dressing.
2. Put in the celery root and apple, and toss to coat well in the dressing. Put in the arugula and walnuts, and toss lightly just to blend. Serve instantly.

CELERY, ARTICHOKE, AND MORTADELLA SALAD

Insalata di Sedano, Carciofi e Mortadella (Italian Name of the Recipe)

Yield: 4 to 6 Servings

Ingredients:

- ½ teaspoon kosher salt
- 3 tablespoons extra-virgin olive oil
- 4 inner celery stalks, with leaves, thinly sliced on the bias

- 8 baby artichokes (approximately 1 pound)
- Juice of 2 lemons, freshly squeezed (save the halves of squeezed lemons)
- One 4-ounce chunk Grana Padano
- One 6-ounce piece mortadella, cut into matchsticks

Directions:

1. Fill a bowl with cold water, put in the juice of 1 lemon and the squeezed-out lemon halves, so you can store the artichokes as you work. Peel and trim the stems from the artichokes. Pull off any tough outer leaves and discard. With a paring knife, trim away any tough parts around the base of each artichoke. Use a serrated knife to cut off the top third of each artichoke and discard. Halve the artichokes and slice along the length very thin, either by hand or on a mandoline. (The artichokes can be sliced crosswise if you prefer.) While you cut, put in the sliced artichokes to the acidulated water. When finished, drain thoroughly, set artichokes in a dry bowl, and toss with the rest of the juice of one lemon.
2. Put in celery to the bowl. On the coarse holes of a box grater, grate most of the chunk of cheese into the bowl, saving for later a small piece for garnish. Sprinkle with the olive oil, and flavor with the salt. Toss thoroughly. Put in the mortadella and toss gently, so as not to break the pieces. Grate rest of the cheese over the top before you serve.

CONDIGGION SALAD WITH TUNA

Condiggion con il Tonno (Italian Name of the Recipe)

Yield: Servings 6

Ingredients:

- ¼ cup chopped fresh Italian parsley
- ¼ cup pitted, chopped oil-cured black olives
- ½ cup fresh basil leaves
- 1 red bell pepper, cut into strips
- 1 small English cucumber, sliced into ¼-inch-thick rounds
- 1 teaspoon kosher salt
- 2 ripe medium tomatoes, cut into 1-inch chunks
- 2 small garlic cloves, crushed and peeled
- 2 teaspoons dried oregano, preferably Sicilian on the branch
- 4 cups 1-inch crustless day-old country-bread cubes
- 6 anchovy fillets
- 7 tablespoons extra-virgin olive oil
- 7 tablespoons red wine vinegar
- Freshly ground black pepper
- Two 5-ounce cans Italian tuna in olive oil, drained

Directions:

1. In a big bowl, sprinkle the bread with ¼ cup of the vinegar and 2 tablespoons olive oil. Put in enough water

(up to ½ cup, depending on how dry the bread is) just to moisten it, and allow it to sit five minutes.
2. In a mini–food processor, mix the garlic, anchovies, basil, and rest of the 3 tablespoons vinegar and 5 tablespoons olive oil. Flavor it with ½ teaspoon of the salt and some black pepper, and process until a smooth dressing is achieved.
3. To the soaked bread, put in the tomatoes, bell pepper, English cucumber, olives, parsley, and oregano. Flavor it with the rest of the ½ teaspoon salt and more black pepper. Toss to cover the vegetables thoroughly in the dressing. Put in the tuna, and toss one more time—lightly, so as not to break up the tuna too much. Serve.

CRAB AND CELERY SALAD

Insalata di Granchio e Sedano (Italian Name of the Recipe)

Yield: Servings 4

Ingredients:

- ¾ teaspoon kosher salt
- 1 pound jumbo lump crabmeat, picked through for shells
- 1½ cups thin bias-cut inner celery stalks and leaves
- 2 big hard-boiled eggs, coarsely chopped
- 2 ripe medium tomatoes, seeded, cut into ½-inch pieces
- 3 tablespoons chopped fresh Italian parsley

- 3 tablespoons extra-virgin olive oil
- 3 tablespoons freshly squeezed lemon juice

Directions:

1. In a big bowl, combine celery, eggs, tomatoes, and parsley. Sprinkle with lemon juice and oil, sprinkle with salt, and toss thoroughly to coat the salad with the dressing. Put in the crabmeat and toss gently to blend, without breaking up the lumps of crab.
2. Serve immediately, or chill for maximum an hour or two.

CUCUMBER, POTATO, AND GREEN BEAN SALAD

Insalata di Cetrioli, Patate e Fagioli Verdi (Italian Name of the Recipe)

Yield: 4 to 6 Servings

Ingredients:

- ⅓ cup extra-virgin olive oil
- ½ medium red onion, thinly sliced
- 1 English cucumber, sliced into ¼-inch-thick half-moons
- 1 pound green beans, trimmed
- 1 teaspoon kosher salt, plus more for the pot
- 3 big red potatoes, cut into 1½-inch chunks (approximately 1¼ pounds)

- 3 tablespoons red wine vinegar
- Freshly ground black pepper

Directions:

1. Bring a big pot of salted water to its boiling point. Put in the potatoes, and simmer until about midway cooked, approximately ten minutes. Put in the green beans and cook until potatoes and beans are soft, approximately five minutes more. Drain in a colander.
2. When the beans are just sufficiently cool to handle (you want them still to be warm for the dressing), Pull each bean apart at the seam into two long pieces, with the seeds uncovered.
3. In a big bowl, whisk together the vinegar and oil and flavor with the salt and pepper. Put in the potatoes, green beans, cucumber, and red onion. Toss thoroughly to coat the vegetables in the dressing, before you serve.

FARRO SALAD WITH GRILLED EGGPLANT AND PEPPERS

Insalata di Farro e Verdure alla Griglia (Italian Name of the Recipe)

Yield: Servings 6

Ingredients:

- ½ cup chopped fresh Italian parsley
- ½ cup extra-virgin olive oil
- 1 big red onion, cut into ½-inch rings
- 1 cup pitted big green olives, quartered
- 1½ cups farro
- 2 fresh bay leaves
- 2 red, yellow, or orange bell peppers, sliced into 1-inch-thick strips
- 2 small Italian eggplants, sliced along the length into ½-inch-thick strips (approximately 1 pound)
- 2 tablespoons pine nuts, toasted
- 2 teaspoons kosher salt, plus more for cooking the farro
- 3 tablespoons white wine vinegar

Directions:

1. Preheat a grill or grill pan on moderate to high heat. Bring a big pot of salted water to its boiling point. Put in the farro and bay leaves. Simmer until farro is tender, approximately twenty to twenty-five minutes. Drain thoroughly, and spread on a sheet pan to cool and dry out while you cook the vegetables. Remove bay leaves from farro.
2. In a big bowl, mix the onion, eggplants, and bell peppers. Toss with 5 tablespoons of the olive oil and 1 teaspoon salt.
3. Grill vegetables, turning once in a while, until lightly charred and tender, approximately five to seven minutes.

4. When all the vegetables are grilled, chop the onion and eggplant into 1-inch pieces; leave the peppers in strips.
5. In a bowl, mix the farro, grilled vegetables, olives, parsley, and pine nuts. Sprinkle with the rest of the 3 tablespoons olive oil, the vinegar, and the rest of the teaspoon of salt. Toss thoroughly to blend. Serve.

LOBSTER SALAD WITH FRESH TOMATOES

Insalata di Aragosta con Pomodori (Italian Name of the Recipe)

Yield: Servings 6 As An Appetizer Or 4 As A Main Course

Ingredients:

- ¼ teaspoon peperoncino, or to taste
- ¾ cup extra-virgin olive oil
- 1 teaspoon kosher salt, plus 6 tablespoons for the lobster pot
- 2 big hard-boiled eggs, chopped
- 2 live lobsters, 1¼ pounds each
- 2 tablespoons chopped fresh Italian parsley
- 3 tender celery stalks with a nice amount of leaves
- 4 ripe tomatoes (approximately 1½ pounds), or 1 pound sweet, ripe cherry tomatoes
- Juice of 2 big lemons, freshly squeezed

Directions:

1. Fill a big stockpot with 6 quarts water, put in 6 tablespoons salt, and bring to a rolling boil. When the water is at a rolling boil, drop in the lobsters and cook them, uncovered, for exactly ten minutes after the water returns to a boil (and then keep it boiling). At the end of ten minutes (or a couple of minutes longer if the lobsters are larger than 1¼ pounds), lift the lobsters from the pot, wash with cold water, drain, and allow them to cool.
2. Core and chop the tomatoes into wedges, approximately 1 inch thick (if you have cherry tomatoes, cut them in half). Cut the celery stalks crosswise into ½-inch pieces, and roughly cut the leaves. Toss the tomatoes and celery together in a big bowl with ½ teaspoon of the salt.
3. When the lobsters are sufficiently cool to handle, twist and pull off the claws and knuckle segments where the knuckles attach to the front of the body. Place the lobsters flat on a cutting board, and cut them in half along the length using a heavy chef's knife. Take the digestive sac, found right behind the eyes, and pull out the vein running along the back of the body and the tail. Cut off the meaty tail piece from the carcass of the four split halves. Take the shell from the upper half of the lobsters, remove the feathered attachments and any surplus skin, and chop the lobster body with small legs attached into three pieces, putting the pieces in a big mixing bowl as you work. It is a good idea to leave the

tomalley and roe in the body pieces, as a special treat while eating the salad. Or you can remove them and discard, if not to your preference.
4. Separate the knuckles from the claws, and crack open the shells of both knuckles and hard claw pincers using the thick edge of the knife blade, or kitchen shears; pull the meat out. Get the meat out of the knuckles too. Chop the tail sections, shell on, crosswise into three pieces each.
5. For the dressing, whisk together the lemon juice, chopped eggs, peperoncino, and rest of the ½ teaspoon salt. Pour in the olive oil in a slow stream, whisking continuously to blend it into a smooth dressing.
6. To serve: Put in the tomatoes and celery to the bowl of lobster pieces. Pour in the dressing, and tumble everything together until uniformly coated. Scatter the parsley on top. Position the salad on a big platter, or compose individual servings on salad plates.

OCTOPUS AND POTATO SALAD

Insalata di Polpo e Patate (Italian Name of the Recipe)

Yield: Servings 6

Ingredients:

- 1 small red onion, thinly sliced
- 2 fresh bay leaves

- 2 medium russet potatoes
- 2 tablespoons chopped fresh Italian parsley
- 3 tablespoons red wine vinegar
- 5 tablespoons extra-virgin olive oil
- Freshly ground black pepper to taste
- Kosher salt to taste
- One 2-to-3-pound octopus, head cleaned

Directions:

1. Put the octopus and bay leaves in a big pot with cold water. Cover, and bring to its boiling point. Reduce the heat, and cook the octopus at a vigorous simmer until soft but a little al dente, approximately forty-five minutes. (Test periodically by inserting the tines of a fork into the thickest part of the octopus. It is done when the fork penetrates easily and is removed with a little resistance.)
2. In the meantime, cover the whole unpeeled potatoes with cold water in a second pot, and bring to its boiling point. Cook until soft, approximately 25 to half an hour, then cool, peel, and cut into 1-inch cubes.
3. Drain the octopus, discarding the bay leaves, and allow it to cool to room temperature. Chop the tentacles away where they join the head, and, if you wish, strip away the skin and suction cups from the tentacles. (It is a good idea to leave the skin and suction cups on.) Clean the inside of the octopus head, which resembles a pouch the

size of your fist, by cutting it in half; then chop the head meat into thin slices. Chop the tentacles into 1-inch pieces, and set the octopus pieces in a bowl with the warm potatoes. Toss thoroughly with the olive oil, red wine vinegar, onion, and parsley. Sprinkle with salt and pepper. Put on a serving platter, decorate with lemon wedges, before you serve.

PICKLED CARROTS

Carote in Agro (Italian Name of the Recipe)

Yield: Servings 6 To 8

Ingredients:

- ½ cup dry white wine
- 1 cup white wine vinegar
- 1 tablespoon extra-virgin olive oil
- 1 tablespoon sugar
- 1 teaspoon kosher salt, plus more for seasoning
- 2 fresh bay leaves
- 3 garlic cloves, crushed and peeled
- 3 sprigs fresh Italian parsley, plus 1 tablespoon chopped
- 3 sprigs fresh mint, plus 1 tablespoon chopped
- 8 bunches baby carrots with tops, peeled and trimmed, with ½ inch of the greens rest of the (about 35 to 40 tiny carrots)

Directions:

1. In a wide deep cooking pan just big enough to hold the carrots in a few layers, mix the vinegar, white wine, sugar, garlic, bay leaves, mint sprigs, parsley sprigs, and 1 teaspoon salt. Bring to a simmer, and put in the carrots and enough water just to cover the carrots, approximately 1 cup. Simmer until carrots are soft— about fifteen minutes, depending on their size. Remove carrots using tongs to a serving dish that will fit them tightly in several layers, strain the cooking liquid over top, and cool to room temperature. Cover, and place in your fridge overnight.
2. Before you serve, bring carrots back to room temperature. Take out of the liquid, and put in to a big bowl. Toss with the olive oil, chopped parsley, chopped mint, and salt to taste. Sprinkle with a few tablespoons of the marinade, just to moisten, before you serve.

POACHED SEAFOOD SALAD

Insalata di Frutti di Mare (Italian Name of the Recipe)

Yield: Servings 6

Ingredients:

For The Court Bouillon

- ½ cup dry white wine

- 1 tablespoon kosher salt
- 1 teaspoon black peppercorns
- 2 celery stalks, trimmed and cut into 1-inch lengths
- 2 medium carrots, peeled and cut into 1-inch lengths
- 4 fresh bay leaves

For The Salad

- ½ cup extra-virgin olive oil
- 1 pound medium (bodies four to 6 inches long) calamari, cleaned, bodies cut into ½-inch rings, tentacles cut in half
- 1 teaspoon chopped garlic
- 1½ pound mussels, scrubbed and debearded
- 12 ounces big shrimp, shells and tails removed, deveined
- 2 tablespoons coarsely chopped fresh Italian parsley
- 2 tablespoons red wine vinegar
- 4 inner celery stalks with leaves, sliced thin (approximately 1½ cups)
- Kosher salt to taste
- Peperoncino to taste

Directions:

1. For the court bouillon: Bring 2 quarts water, the wine, celery, carrots, bay leaves, peppercorns, and salt to its boiling point in a wide casserole or frying pan. Regulate the heat to simmering, cover, and cook ten minutes.
2. Put in the shrimp to the court bouillon, and cook them until they are barely opaque in the center, approximately

4 minutes. Fish the shrimp out with a spider, and spread them out on a baking sheet. It is okay if they aren't completely drained—you'll use some of the liquid to finish the salad. Put in the calamari, and poach just until they are firm and tender, approximately two to three minutes. Fish out the calamari, and put in them to the shrimp.

3. Return the court bouillon to its boiling point. Mix in the mussels, cover the pot, and cook until the shells open and the mussels are firm but not tough, approximately 4 minutes. Remove with a skimmer and put in to the other poached seafood. Reserve half a cup of the cooking liquid. When the mussels are sufficiently cool, pluck the meat from the shells directly into a big serving bowl.

4. For the salad, transfer the cooled shrimp and calamari to the bowl with the mussels, shaking off peppercorns as you do. Put in the celery, parsley, and garlic, then pour in the olive oil and vinegar. Toss until combined, drizzling in the reserved cooking liquid. Season the salad to taste with salt and peperoncino. The salad must be very moist and glisten with dressing. If not, put in a dash of olive oil and vinegar. Let the salad stand at room temperature about half an hour, tossing a couple of times. Check the seasoning, and toss thoroughly just before you serve.

PUNTARELLE AND ANCHOVY SALAD

Insalata di Puntarelle e Acciughe (Italian Name of the Recipe)

Yield: Servings 4

Ingredients:

- 1 pound puntarelle
- 2 tablespoons extra-virgin olive oil
- 2 tablespoons red wine vinegar
- 4 anchovy fillets, coarsely chopped
- 4 ounces dried cannellini or other white beans, soaked in water overnight
- Kosher salt and freshly ground black pepper

Directions:

1. Clean the puntarelle, separate the outer green leaves from the center, and cook them in boiling water until soft, approximately twenty minutes. In the meantime, chop the center and the small asparaguslike tips into fine strips (2 by ¼ inches) and allow it to sit in ice water for about two hours.
2. In the meantime, drain the soaked beans and transfer them to a big deep cooking pan. Pour in enough cold water to cover the beans liberally. Bring to its boiling point, regulate the heat to a simmer, and cook until the beans are soft, approximately forty minutes.
3. When all is cooked and cooled, whisk together the oil, vinegar, salt, and pepper in a moderate-sized bowl. Chop

the boiled green leaves into pieces, and place them in a moderate-sized bowl. Put in the cooked beans and half of the dressing. Toss thoroughly. Put in anchovies to rest of the dressing and mix, toss in drained puntarelle center and tips, and toss thoroughly.
4. To serve: set the dressed cooked puntarelle and beans on a plate, and top with uncooked dressed puntarelle center and tips.

RADICCHIO SALAD WITH ORANGE

Insalata di Radicchio e Arancia (Italian Name of the Recipe)

Yield: 4 to 6 Servings

Ingredients:

- 2 navel oranges
- Juice of 1 lemon, freshly squeezed
- 2 teaspoons Dijon mustard
- 1 teaspoon kosher salt
- Freshly ground black pepper
- ¼ cup extra-virgin olive oil
- 2 heads radicchio, coarsely chopped (approximately eight cups)
- 1 cup thinly sliced radishes
- ¼ cup pitted oil-cured black olives, coarsely chopped

Directions:

1. Chop the top and bottom from an orange, so it sits upright on your cutting board. Cut down, following the shape of the orange, to remove the peel and white pith, leaving only the flesh of the orange. To section the oranges: hold the orange in your hand and cut out the segments, leaving the membrane behind. Put the segments in a big serving bowl, and squeeze any juice from the membrane into a moderate-sized bowl. Repeat with the rest of the orange.
2. To the moderate-sized bowl with the orange juice, put in the lemon juice, mustard, salt, and pepper. Whisk to blend. Whisk in the olive oil in a slow, steady stream to make a smooth, fairly dense dressing.
3. To the bowl with the orange segments, put in the radicchio, radishes, and olives. Sprinkle with the dressing, and toss thoroughly. Serve.

RAW AND COOKED SALAD

Insalata Cotta e Cruda (Italian Name of the Recipe)

Yield: Servings 6

Ingredients:

- ½ cup extra-virgin olive oil, plus more as required
- ½ cup pitted black olives

- ½ teaspoon kosher salt, plus more as required
- 1 or 2 fresh ripe tomatoes (approximately eight ounces), cored and cut into wedges
- 1 or 2 heads Bibb lettuce (approximately 12 ounces), leaves torn, washed, and dried
- 1 pound sweet onions, such as Vidalia or Walla Walla
- 12 ounces red-bliss potatoes, medium in size
- 3 tablespoons drained tiny capers in brine
- 3 tablespoons red wine vinegar
- 8 ounces green beans, trimmed
- Freshly ground black pepper to taste

Directions:

1. For the *verdura cotta* (cooked vegetables): Preheat your oven to 375 degrees. Peel and trim the onions and slice into rounds about ¾ inch thick. Brush with some of the olive oil, and drizzle salt lightly on both sides. Place the onions on a baking sheet, and roast for about twenty minutes or longer, until a little softened and nicely caramelized. Cool, then separate the rounds into rings.
2. In the meantime, drop the potatoes—whole, with skin on—into a pot with sufficient water. Bring to a gentle boil, and cook just until a sharp knife blade slides through the potatoes. Take out using a skimmer, and chop the potatoes into wedges approximately 1½ inches thick.
3. When the potatoes are out of the boiling water, drop the green beans in and cook until al dente, around four

minutes or so. Drain, and drop the beans into ice water, to set the color. Once they're chilled, drain and dry the beans, and cut into 2-inch lengths.

4. Mix the cooked vegetables in a big serving bowl with the olives, capers, and tomatoes. Drizzle with the rest of the salt and some freshly ground pepper, sprinkle the rest of the olive oil and the red wine vinegar over vegetables, and tumble them to coat with dressing. Scatter the lettuce on top, then toss to distribute the dressing uniformly. Serve instantly.

RED CABBAGE AND BACON SALAD

Insalata di Cappuccio Rosso e Pancetta (Italian Name of the Recipe)

Yield: 4 to 6 Servings

Ingredients:

- ¼ cup extra-virgin olive oil
- 1 pound sliced bacon, cut into 1-inch pieces
- 1 small head red cabbage
- 5 tablespoons balsamic vinegar
- Kosher salt

Directions:

1. Clean and remove the tough outer leaves of the cabbage, cut in half, and cut out the core. Thinly shred the red

cabbage, by hand or on a mandoline (preferred), into a big bowl.
2. Heat 1 tablespoon olive oil in a big frying pan on moderate heat. Cook the bacon until crisp, approximately five to six minutes, then remove to a paper-towel-lined plate. Pour off most of the fat, and return the pan to the heat.
3. Put in the rest of the olive oil and the vinegar to the frying pan. Bring the liquid to an energetic simmer, and pour the hot sauce over the cabbage in the bowl. Mop out the frying pan with a handful of the cabbage to get the crusty bits from the bottom of the pan, and put in to the bowl. Put in the cooked bacon, flavor with the salt, and toss thoroughly so the cabbage doesn't stick together. Serve warm.

ROASTED BEET AND BEET GREENS SALAD WITH APPLES AND GOAT CHEESE

Insalata di Barbabietole con Mele e Formaggio di Capra (Italian Name of the Recipe)

Yield: Servings 6

Ingredients:

- ⅓ cup extra-virgin olive oil
- ⅓ cup good-quality balsamic vinegar

- ½ teaspoon kosher salt
- 1 medium tart, crisp apple (such as Granny Smith), cut into matchsticks (peel on)
- 10-12 small yellow and red beets with greens attached (about 3 pounds total)
- 4 ounces or so a little aged goat cheese
- Freshly ground black pepper

Directions:

1. Preheat your oven to 400 degrees. Take the beet greens, leaving about an inch of stem on the beets, and poke each beet using a fork a few times. Put the beets in a shallow roasting pan with approximately an inch of water, uncovered. Roast until soft all the way through, approximately forty-five minutes to 1 hour. Allow to cool. (The beets can also be boiled whole and unpeeled, if you don't want to heat the oven, but they taste better when baked.)
2. Bring a big deep cooking pan of salted water to its boiling point. Wash the greens, and trim off any very tough parts of the stems or blemishes on the leaves. Trim the softer stems, and keep separate from the leaves. Put in the stems to the boiling water and cook ten minutes. Put in the leaves and cook until all is very tender, approximately fifteen to twenty minutes. Drain thoroughly, and flavor with ¼ teaspoon salt. Allow to cool.

3. Peel the beets, and cut into 2-inch wedges. Chop the greens and stems into 2-inch pieces. Put all in a big bowl.
4. In a small bowl, whisk together the olive oil and vinegar, and flavor with the rest of the salt and some pepper. Toss the dressing with the beets and greens. Put in the apples at the last minute, so as not to discolor them too much, and toss all once more. Spread on serving plates or a platter, and crumble the goat cheese over all.

ROASTED EGGPLANT AND TOMATO SALAD

Insalata di Melanzane e Pomodori Arrostiti (Italian Name of the Recipe)

Yield: Servings 6

Ingredients:

- ¼ cup red wine vinegar
- ¼ teaspoon freshly ground black pepper
- ⅓ cup shredded fresh mozzarella or ricotta salata
- ½ teaspoon kosher salt, plus more to taste
- 12 small fresh basil leaves, or 2 tablespoons shredded big fresh basil leaves
- 2 medium eggplants (approximately 1¼ pounds)
- 3 cups ripe grape or small cherry tomatoes
- 4 tablespoons extra-virgin olive oil

Directions:

1. Preheat your oven to 450 degrees. Trim the ends of the eggplants and slice crosswise into 1-inch-thick rounds; cut each round into halves or quarters, to make more or less identical pieces smaller than 2 inches on a side. Put the chunks on a baking sheet coated with parchment, and drizzle over them 1 tablespoon oil and ¼ teaspoon salt. Toss thoroughly.
2. Put the tomatoes on a separate parchment-lined sheet pan, drizzle over them 1 tablespoon oil and a pinch of salt, roll them around, and spread them out. Put both sheets in the oven, and roast until both the eggplant and the tomatoes are soft, shriveled, and nicely caramelized on the edges, half an hour or more. Turn the eggplant chunks a couple of times while roasting, roll the tomatoes over, and shift the sheets around in the oven for uniform heating.
3. Let the vegetables cool to room temperature on the sheets, then transfer to a big mixing bowl. Toss gently with the rest of the 2 tablespoons olive oil, ¼ teaspoon salt, some ground pepper, the vinegar, and basil. Taste, and calibrate the seasonings. Position the salad on a serving platter or portion on salad plates, and drizzle the shredded cheese on top.

SALAD OF DANDELION GREENS WITH ALMOND VINAIGRETTE AND DRIED RICOTTA

Insalata di Cicoria con Vinaigrette di Mandorle e Ricotta Salata (Italian Name of the Recipe)

Yield: Servings 6

Ingredients:

- ¼ cup sliced almonds, toasted
- ¼ pound ricotta salata, shaved into shards with a vegetable peeler
- 1 pound tender young dandelion greens (approximately 10 loosely packed cups)
- 1 teaspoon honey
- 2 tablespoons red wine vinegar
- 6 tablespoons extra-virgin olive oil
- Kosher salt and freshly ground black pepper

Directions:

1. Cut tough stems from the greens, and remove any wilted, yellow, or tough leaves. Rinse and dry thoroughly. The greens can be prepared up to several hours in advance and kept, loosely covered with a clean towel, in your fridge.

2. To make the dressing: Mix the olive oil, 2 tablespoons of the toasted almonds, the vinegar, and honey in a blender, and blend until the desired smoothness is achieved. Put in salt and pepper to taste. Put the greens in a big bowl, season them with salt and pepper, and pour the dressing over them. Toss thoroughly, and split the dressed greens among six plates, mounding them in the center of the plates. Drizzle with the rest of the 2 tablespoons of toasted almonds, and top with shavings of ricotta salata. Serve instantly.

SCALLION AND ASPARAGUS SALAD

Insalata di Scalogna e Asparagi (Italian Name of the Recipe)

Yield: Servings 6

Ingredients:

- 1 big bunch fresh asparagus (approximately 12 ounces)
- 1 bunch scallions
- 1 teaspoon kosher salt
- 1½ tablespoons red wine vinegar
- 3 hard-boiled eggs
- 3½ tablespoons extra-virgin olive oil
- Freshly ground black pepper

Directions:

1. Use a vegetable peeler to shave off the skin from the bottom 3 inches or so of each asparagus stalk, so they cook uniformly. Detach the hard stubs at the bottom—they'll break naturally at the correct spot as you bend the bottom of the asparagus. To prepare the scallions: Trim the roots and the wilted ends of the green leaves. Peel off the loose layers at the white end, so the scallions are all trim.
2. Bring 1 quart water (or enough to cover the vegetables) to its boiling point in a wide, deep frying pan, and put in the asparagus and scallions. Regulate the heat to maintain a bubbling boil, and poach the vegetables, uncovered, for approximately 6 minutes at least, until they become soft but not falling apart, thoroughly cooked but not mushy. To check doneness, pick up an asparagus spear by its middle using tongs: it must be a little droopy, but not collapsing.
3. Once they are done, lift out the vegetables using tongs and lay them in a colander. Hold the colander under cold running water to stop the cooking. Drain for a short time, then spread on kitchen towels, pat dry, and drizzle ½ teaspoon salt over them.
4. Chop the asparagus and the scallions into 1-inch lengths, and pile them loosely in a mixing bowl. Sprinkle the oil and vinegar over the top, and drizzle on the rest of the salt and several grinds of black pepper. Toss thoroughly. Quarter the eggs into wedges, and slice each wedge into two or three pieces; scatter these in the bowl, and fold in

with the vegetables. Taste, and tweak the dressing. Serve at room temperature, or chill the salad for a short period of time; position it on a serving platter or on salad plates.

SEAFOOD AND RICE SALAD

Insalata di Riso e Frutti di Mare (Italian Name of the Recipe)

Yield: Servings 6

Ingredients:

For The Rice

- 1 teaspoon kosher salt
- 1½ cups long-grain rice
- 2 fresh bay leaves
- 2 tablespoons extra-virgin olive oil

For The Seafood

- ¼ teaspoon crushed red pepper flakes
- ½ teaspoon kosher salt
- 1 cup dry white wine
- 12 littleneck clams, scrubbed
- 2 pounds mussels, scrubbed and debearded
- 2 tablespoons extra-virgin olive oil
- 3 garlic cloves, peeled and sliced
- 8 ounces big shrimp, peeled and deveined

- 8 ounces medium calamari, cleaned, tubes cut into ½-inch rings, head with tentacles cut in half
- Peel of 1 big lemon, removed with a vegetable peeler (reserve the lemon)

For The Salad

- ½ medium red onion, sliced
- 1 medium fennel bulb, halved, cored, and thinly sliced, plus ½ cup chopped fronds
- 1 teaspoon kosher salt
- 2 celery stalks, thinly sliced on the bias
- 3 tablespoons chopped fresh Italian parsley
- 3 tablespoons extra-virgin olive oil
- Juice of 1 lemon (peel used in cooking seafood)

Directions:

1. For the rice: In a moderate-sized deep cooking pan, combine 3 cups water, the bay leaves, olive oil, and salt. Bring to its boiling point. Put in the rice, decrease the heat to a simmer, cover the pot, and simmer fifteen minutes without opening the lid. Turn off the heat, allow it to stand five minutes, and fluff the rice using a fork. Spread rice onto a sheet pan to cool, and discard the bay leaves.
2. For the seafood: In a big Dutch oven, heat the olive oil on moderate to high heat. When the oil is hot, put in the garlic and lemon peel, and let sizzle one minute. Sprinkle

with salt and red pepper flakes, and put in the wine. Bring to a simmer, put in the clams, and cover the pot. Let steam two minutes; then put in the mussels. Cover, and simmer until most of the clams and mussels open, approximately 4 minutes more. Remove open clams and mussels to a bowl using tongs. Cover, and give the last few another couple of minutes to steam. Put in any more open ones to the bowl, and discard any that refuse to open.
3. Return the cooking liquid to a simmer, and put in the calamari. Simmer just until the calamari curls and turns white (don't overcook!), approximately two minutes, and remove using tongs to a big serving bowl. Put in the shrimp to the pot, and simmer just until they turn pink, approximately 4 minutes. Put in to the bowl with the calamari.
4. Pluck the clams and mussels from the shells, and put in to the serving bowl with the calamari and shrimp. Strain the cooking juices, and save for later.
5. For the salad: In a moderate-sized bowl, whisk together ½ cup cooking juices, the olive oil, lemon juice, chopped parsley, and fennel fronds. Sprinkle with salt.
6. To the serving bowl with the seafood, put in the celery, sliced fennel, and red onion along with the rice. Sprinkle all with the dressing, and toss thoroughly to blend, adding a little more of the cooking juices if the salad seems dry. Serve.

SHAVED FENNEL, CELERY, AND RED ONION SALAD WITH SALAMI

Insalata di Finocchio, Sedano, Cipolla e Salame (Italian Name of the Recipe)

Yield: 4 to 6 Servings

Ingredients:

- ¼ cup extra-virgin olive oil
- ½ medium red onion, thinly sliced
- ½ teaspoon kosher salt
- 1 big fennel bulb, trimmed and thinly sliced crosswise (about 4 cups), plus ½ cup chopped fronds (use a mandoline, if you have one, to shave the fennel)
- 3 big celery stalks, trimmed, peeled, and thinly sliced on the bias
- 4 ounces caciocavallo or smoked mozzarella cheese, julienned
- 4 ounces salami, thickly sliced and julienned
- Freshly ground black pepper
- Juice of 1 big lemon, freshly squeezed

Directions:

1. In a big bowl, mix the fennel (but not the fronds), celery, red onion, salami, and cheese.
2. Sprinkle with the lemon juice and olive oil, and flavor with the salt and some pepper. Toss thoroughly to coat

all of the ingredients with the dressing. Drizzle with the chopped fennel fronds and toss lightly. Let sit about ten minutes before you serve, to mix the flavors.

SHRIMP AND MIXED BEAN SALAD

Insalata di Gamberetti e Fagioli Misti (Italian Name of the Recipe)

Yield: Servings 6

Ingredients:

- ¼ teaspoon kosher salt, plus more for the pot
- ½ small onion
- 1 celery stalk, diced
- 1 pound big shrimp, peeled and deveined
- 1 pound fresh or frozen fava beans, shelled
- 1 pound freshly shelled borlotti beans
- 1 small carrot, peeled and sliced
- 2 fresh bay leaves
- 3 tablespoons extra-virgin olive oil
- 3 tablespoons red wine vinegar
- Freshly ground black pepper to taste

Directions:

1. Bring a big deep cooking pan of salted water to its boiling point. Cook the borlotti beans until soft, approximately eight minutes, and then cook the fava beans for about

four minutes. Drain, refresh the beans under cold running water as they finish cooking, and remove the outer skins from the favas.
2. In a moderate-sized deep cooking pan, boil the onion, bay leaves, carrot, and celery in 6 cups water for about twenty minutes. Put in the shrimp, and cook just until opaque throughout, approximately two minutes. Remove and drain the shrimp, and allow them to cool. In a serving bowl, whisk together the olive oil, vinegar, and salt and pepper. Put in the beans and shrimp, and toss to coat completely with the dressing. Serve warm.

STEAMED BROCCOLI AND EGG SALAD

Insalata di Broccoli al Vapore con Uova Sode (Italian Name of the Recipe)

Yield: 4 to 6 Servings

Ingredients:

- ½ teaspoon kosher salt, plus more for the pot
- 1 big head broccoli (approximately 1½ pounds)
- 2 hard-boiled eggs, cut into wedges
- 2 tablespoons extra-virgin olive oil
- 2 tablespoons red wine vinegar

Directions:

1. Peel the lower stem and the head of the broccoli and cut in ¼-inch rounds. Bring a big pot of salted water to its boiling point. Put in the broccoli, bring back to its boiling point, and cook until soft but al dente, approximately eight to ten minutes. Drain and let cool.
2. In a big bowl, whisk together the olive oil, vinegar, and salt. Put in the broccoli, and toss to coat with the dressing. Mound into a serving bowl, and top with the egg wedges. Sprinkle with any rest of the dressing left in the bowl. Serve instantly. (For a more homogeneous salad, chop the eggs into eighths and toss with the broccoli and dressing.)

STRIPED BASS SALAD

Insalata di Branzino (Italian Name of the Recipe)

Yield: Servings 4

Ingredients:

- ¼ cup extra-virgin olive oil
- ½ medium red onion, thinly sliced
- 1 English cucumber, sliced into ½-inch-thick half-moons
- 1 medium carrot, peeled and sliced
- 1 small onion, sliced
- 1½ teaspoons kosher salt
- 2 fresh bay leaves
- 2 pounds skinless striped-bass (or other firm fish) fillet

- 2 tablespoons chopped fresh Italian parsley
- 2 tablespoons white wine vinegar
- 3 tablespoons red wine vinegar
- Freshly ground black pepper

Directions:

1. In a big pot, bring 3 quarts water to its boiling point with the bay leaves, onion, carrot, white wine vinegar, and 1 teaspoon salt. Simmer fifteen minutes. Tie the fish fillets so they lie flat in cheesecloth. Put in the fish to the liquid, and adjust the heat so it is barely simmering. Cook until fish is just thoroughly cooked, approximately ten minutes, depending on the thickness of the fillet. Take the fish to a plate, cool to room temperature, still in the cheesecloth, then place in your fridge until chilled.
2. Take the fish from the cheesecloth and flake in big pieces into a serving bowl. Put in the cucumber, red onion, and parsley. Sprinkle with the red wine vinegar and oil, and flavor with the rest of the ½ teaspoon salt and some black pepper. Lightly toss just to blend. Serve.

TOMATO AND BREAD SALAD

Panzanella (Italian Name of the Recipe)

Yield: Servings 6

Ingredients:

- 1 cup coarsely diced red onion
- 1 pound two-day-old country-style bread, crusts removed, cut into ½-inch cubes (approximately eight cups)
- 12 fresh basil leaves, shredded, plus a few extra sprigs for garnish
- 2 pounds ripe tomatoes at room temperature, cored, seeded, and cut into ½-inch cubes (about 4 cups)
- 3 tablespoons red wine vinegar
- 5 tablespoons extra-virgin olive oil
- Kosher salt and freshly ground black pepper

Directions:

1. Toss the bread, tomatoes, onion, and shredded basil leaves in a big bowl until thoroughly combined. Sprinkle the olive oil and vinegar over the salad, and toss to mix thoroughly. (If bread is overly dry and hard, drizzle with warm water and let it steep for fifteen minutes; then make the salad.)
2. Sprinkle salt and pepper to taste, and allow it to stand ten minutes before you serve. Garnish with sprigs of fresh basil.

TRIPE SALAD

Insalata di Trippa (Italian Name of the Recipe)

Yield: Servings 4

Ingredients:

- 1 garlic clove, finely chopped
- 1 small onion, halved
- 1 teaspoon kosher salt, plus more for the pot
- 2 fresh bay leaves
- 2 pounds honeycomb tripe
- 2 tablespoons chopped fresh Italian parsley
- 3 tablespoons white wine vinegar
- 5 tablespoons extra-virgin olive oil
- 6 black peppercorns
- Freshly ground black pepper

Directions:

1. Put the tripe in a big pot. Put in cold water to cover by 2 inches and the bay leaves, onion, peppercorns, and a generous pinch of salt. Bring to a simmer, and cook until the tripe is tender all the way through when pierced using a fork in the thickest part, approximately 1 to 1½ hours. Drain and cool the tripe.
2. Chop the tripe into 2-by-2-inch pieces. Turn the pieces honeycomb side down, and scrape away any fat or membranes. Cut tripe pieces into julienne strips, and put in to a big serving bowl.

3. In a small bowl, whisk together the vinegar, garlic, salt, and some pepper. Whisk in the olive oil. Sprinkle the dressing over the salad, drizzle with the parsley, and toss thoroughly. Serve.

WARM MUSHROOM SALAD

Insalata di Funghi Tiepida (Italian Name of the Recipe)

Yield: 4 to 6 Servings

Ingredients:

- 1 bunch scallions, trimmed and chopped (approximately 1 cup)
- 1 teaspoon chopped fresh thyme
- 1¼ teaspoons kosher salt
- 2 pounds mixed fresh wild mushrooms, thickly sliced (cremini, shiitake, porcini, oyster, chanterelle)
- 3 medium heads frisée, trimmed into bite-sized pieces, or 8 ounces baby kale or spinach
- 3 tablespoons red wine vinegar
- 4 ounces pancetta, diced
- 5 tablespoons extra-virgin olive oil
- One 2-ounce chunk Grana Padano

Directions:

1. To a big frying pan on moderate to high heat, put in 3 tablespoons of the olive oil and the pancetta. Cook until

the pancetta is crisp, approximately 4 minutes, then remove it to drain on paper towels.
2. Put in the mushrooms to the fat left in the pan. Flavor it with the thyme and 1 teaspoon of the salt. Cover and cook, letting the mushrooms release their juices, approximately three minutes. Uncover, increase the heat to high, and cook until the liquid in the pan is gone and the mushrooms are browned all over, approximately 6 minutes. Put in the scallions, and cook until wilted, approximately three minutes. Scrape the contents of the pan into a big serving bowl, and let cool five minutes.
3. Once the mushrooms are a little cool, put in the frisée and the reserved pancetta, and sprinkle with the vinegar and rest of the 2 tablespoons olive oil. Flavor it with the rest of the ¼ teaspoon salt, and toss thoroughly. Mound on serving plates and, using a vegetable peeler, shave some Grana Padano over each serving. Serve instantly.

Endnote

Thank you for the time you spent on my book. I hope this book has added at least a few Italian recipes to your cooking arsenal.

Good Luck, Have Fun, and Happy Cooking!

Printed in Great Britain
by Amazon